Frederick A. P. (Frederick Augustus Porter) Barnard

The imaginary metrological system of the Great pyramid of Gizeh;

Frederick A. P. (Frederick Augustus Porter) Barnard
The imaginary metrological system of the Great pyramid of Gizeh;
ISBN/EAN: 9783742850539

Manufactured in Europe, USA, Canada, Australia, Japa

Cover: Foto ©Andreas Hilbeck / pixelio.de

Manufactured and distributed by brebook publishing software (www.brebook.com)

Frederick A. P. (Frederick Augustus Porter) Barnard

The imaginary metrological system of the Great pyramid of Gizeh;

PREFACE.

AMONG the many vagaries of the human mind which history records, there is not one more extraordinary than that which has been busying itself for the last twenty years in weaving a network of religious mystery around the Great Pyramid of Gizeh. If it were not a law of fanaticism that the faith of its subjects and victims is intense in proportion as its foundations are weak, and that its disciples multiply in proportion as its doctrines are defiant of common sense, it might reasonably have been expected that the wild conjectures in regard to this monument hazarded by John Taylor in 1859 would have fallen unnoticed from the press, and would long since have ceased to be remembered among men.

It is a fact, nevertheless, that this strange fantasy has been adopted as the creed of a numerous and actively militant sect, who, not content with cherishing their favorite hallucination among themselves, have found in it the inciting motive of a crusade against the spirit of progress of the age; and under the pretext that the imperfect system of weights and measures in common use among us is a system derived from the Pyramid, and divinely appointed, which it would be sacrilege to touch even for the removal of its defects, have attempted the quixotic task of turning back the wheels of a beneficent revolution which has, within the last half century, spread itself over the larger part of the Christian world.

The essay embraced in the following pages is a reprint of a paper contributed, in the ordinary course of business, to the Proceedings of the American Metrological Society, in December, 1883, and published immediately thereafter in the SCHOOL OF MINES QUARTERLY of Columbia College. The object for which that Association was founded was not, as the devotees of the Pyramid faith have industriously represented, to secure the introduction of the Metric System of Weights and Measures into the United States. It was to promote inquiry into the history and principles of Metrological Science in general; and although the majority of its members favor the Metric System, others are little interested in that subject, while among those who earliest enrolled themselves upon its list, were some who had been the public opponents of that system. It invites and willingly receives arguments on either side of the question; and it offers impartially to advocates and opponents alike such opportunities of publication as its Proceedings afford.

The publication of this essay in the present form has not been sought by the Society. It has been yielded to the request of the publishers, who have believed that the discussion which it contains would not be without interest to the general public.

F. A. P. BARNARD.

COLUMBIA COLLEGE, *April*, 1884.

THE METROLOGY OF THE GREAT PYRAMID.

IN every stage of society, even the rudest, the interchange between individuals of articles of personal property has been going on from the earliest time. Very imperfect notions, however, were originally entertained of the relative value of the objects thus exchanged. The esteem in which they were held had been, of course, dependent upon their properties—but properties so widely different as those of practical utility and empty ornament. In the earliest transactions of the primitive races, articles of barter were probably transferred by tale, and *number* constituted the only measure of quantity. But as advancing civilization brought with it juster notions of economy, the desire of each individual to secure the largest returns for the labor of his hands, or for his diligence in the chase, led to closer scrutiny of the terms of every transaction of bargain and sale, and thus created a demand for the means of ascertaining with some approach to exactness, the amounts of merchandise transferred. In some cases the questions thus arising concerned length, in others weight, and in others bulk. In regard to length, reference was naturally made to the dimensions of some part of the human person, as being always present for verification. Hence the use of such measures as the foot, the ell (*ulna*, the elbow, *i. e.*, the fore-arm), the cubit (*cubitus*, of similar signification), the yard (*geard, gyrd*, the girdle), the digit (*digitus*, finger, *i. e.*, a finger's breadth), etc., etc. For weight and bulk, such natural standards do not present themselves. It was necessary to adopt units arbitrary in their character; and as the magnitude of these units would be determined by the uses they would be required most frequently to subserve in the ordinary business of life, it has happened that, though many have originated among different peoples, independently of each other, there has been everywhere an approximation to a common mean value. Thus the unit of weight has been found, for the most part, to vary between five and ten thousand English grains troy; though in a limited number of instances it has fallen outside of these limits. Similar variations have been found in the leading units of capacity. It has only been when, in the progress of enlightenment, systems of metrology have been formed on scientific principles, that units of weight and measure have been connected with, and made dependent on, units of length. In the earlier stages of society, commercial exchanges between different countries, and even between different provinces, towns and villages of the same country, were infrequent and of comparatively insignificant importance. Each small community, therefore, originated its own system of weights and measures; and the total number of such systems simultaneously existing, has always, down to the middle of the present century, been excessively great. Some idea of this diversity may be formed from an examination of the tables presented to the Society some time since, and printed in Barnard's Metric System, published in 1879 in Boston, of the values given to a particular weight and a particular measure similarly named throughout Europe and the countries colonized by Europeans, and known as the pound weight (*pondus*, or *libra ponderis*), and the foot measure ($\pi o\acute{u}s$, pes, pé, pié, pied, fuss, fot, fod, foot), in which will be found no fewer than three hundred and ninety-one different pound weights, and two hundred and ninety-two different foot measures; all, with the exception of two or three, derived from antiquity, in actual use, somewhere or another, at the close of the eighteenth century.

It was in the hope of removing the confusion, and remedying the inconvenience to all mankind occasioned by this multiplicity of the forms of expressing the quantities of exchangeable commodities, that in the years preceding the outburst of revolutionary violence in France, and while the king was still on the throne, overtures were made to the British Government by King Louis XVI., at the instance of the Constituent Assembly, inviting the appointment of a joint committee of members of the Royal Society of London and of the French Academy of Sciences, to agree upon some natural standard of length as a basis of an universal system of weights and measures. This was the first step in a movement which culminated in the adoption, on the 22d of June, 1789, by an international commission called to meet at Paris, and composed of delegates of ten independent States, of the ten-millionth part of the quadrant of the Paris meridian, under the name of the metre, as the basic unit of a new and improved system of weights and measures. The system founded upon this base, and called therefore the metric system, has, in subsequent years, been generally adopted by civilized nations. Those which have hitherto failed to accept it are England, the United States, and Russia; but even in these countries, its use has become general among scientific men.

Very decisive indications make it evident that the introduction of this system for exclusive use in all these countries is only a question of time. In Russia, the use of the system in the custom houses was ordered as early as 1870. In 1876, an Imperial Commission sent to Paris to inquire into the operation of the system in Western and Central Europe, made on its return a favorable report. In the British House of Commons, in 1868, a bill making the use of the system compulsory, after a time to be fixed by the Government, passed its second reading by a heavy majority, but was not put upon its final passage, in consequence of a representation by the ministry that it would be judicious, before further action, to await the report of a commission previously appointed by the crown, to inquire into the state of the standards, and to advise as to the legislation needed in regard to them. This commission reported, in 1869, as their "unanimous conclusion," that " the best course is cautiously but steadily to introduce the metric system into this country." In 1871, a bill making the system compulsory in England after a limited term of years, was again introduced into Parliament; but a number of influences conspired to make the occasion inopportune, and it was not pressed to a vote.

In our own country, the permissive use of the system was sanctioned by act of Congress in 1866. Early in 1879, a report of the Committee on Coinage, Weights and Measures, of the House of Representatives, signed unanimously, recommended the use of the system in the post-offices and custom-houses of the United States; and a bill designed to give effect to that recommendation was introduced. Unfortunately, the report was made so late as February to a Congress about to expire by limitation on the fourth of March, and time did not allow its consideration. The States of Connecticut, Massachusetts and New Jersey have, by their legislation, favored the introduction of the system, and have provided that its principles shall be taught in the public schools.

From evidences like these, it must be manifest to every thinking man that a system which has already been so widely accepted as a means of regulating the ordinary transactions of business between man and man in every-day life, and which is involved in the greater part of the international commerce of the human race, must sooner or later be universally prevalent. Some time may yet elapse before this anticipation is realized, as the absurd system of metrology now in existence among us gives token that it is not likely to die easily. In this country the opposition has even been organized, and an "Institute" has been established, calling itself "International," and professing to be designed "for preserving and perfecting weights and measures," which, during the past three or four years, has been flooding this country with its circulars, and bombarding Congress with its petitions. This agitation may not be without some temporary effect, especially in the way of scaring politicians, who are always frightened by clamor of any kind, whether accompanied by sense or not; but in its influence upon the great and steady march of public opinion, its ultimate effect will be about equal to that produced by the honest old lady who attempted to sweep back the rising tide of the Atlantic with a broom.

A favorite argument with the association above named, and of the simple-minded enthusiasts who, in this country and in Great Britain, concur in the views which it advocates, is that the weights and measures now in use among us are an *inheritance* received by us from those early generations among which God himself condescended to be the immediate ruler of his chosen people; that they were directly prescribed by Him to Moses or the earlier patriarchs, and, therefore, that to prefer any others before them is an act not of folly merely, but of sin. This doctrine has grown out of some curious speculations as to the principles which governed the construction of the great pyramid of Cheops, at Gizeh, and the purposes for which that huge and senseless pile was constructed. It is asserted that this mysterious structure is the material embodiment of a mass of scientific truth which has hitherto been supposed to have become known to the human race only in comparatively recent times; and which was perhaps not known to the builders themselves, but was incorporated into their work through a divine guidance, which they unconsciously obeyed. And the object, it is claimed, for which the supreme ruler of the universe impelled these, his agents, to erect this massive and costly monument was merely to perpetuate to coming generations a knowledge of the weights and measures which he had himself given to his chosen people as early as the Exodus, or probably earlier. The originator—he regarded himself as the discoverer, but we should rather incline to consider him the ingenious inventor—of this singular theory, was John Taylor, of London, a man of intelligence and of some pretensions to science, who, in 1859, published a book entitled "The Great Pyramid: Why it was built, and who built it?" The second question embraced in this title is, after an elaborate inquiry, thus answered by the author: "Omitting HAM and his descendants, and leaving it doubtful whether JAPHETH, or any of his family, were engaged in this great undertaking, we have for the probable founders of the Pyramid: 1, NOAH; 2, SHEM; 3, ARPHAXAD and his brethren, *Elam, Ashur, Lud* and *Aram;* 4, SALAH and his cousins, *Uz, Hul, Gether* and *Mash;* 5, EBER; 6, PELEG and his brother, JOKTAN; 7, REU and his cousins, the THIRTEEN SONS OF JOKTAN; by some of whom, if not by all, was commenced, carried on, and completed the most magnificent, disinterested, and glorious work that was ever conceived and executed by mankind." He adds: "To NOAH we must ascribe the original idea, the presiding mind, and the benevolent purpose. He who built the ark was, of all men, the most competent to direct the building of the Great Pyramid." There seems to be something bordering on the ludicrous in the ascription to a man situated as Noah was at that time—a man just escaped from a catastrophe so frightful as the destruction of the whole human race, his own immediate family only excepted—there is something approaching sublimity in the absurdity of ascribing to a man in circumstances so forlorn—left companionless, helpless, almost alone, to begin anew the battle of life amid the wreck of a ruined world—a project, so wild, so cyclopean, so almost stupidly idiotic, as that of heaping up a pile of massive rock a million and a half cubic yards in volume, and, according to the calculations of Professor Piazzi Smyth, more than five and a quarter millions of pyramid tons, and exceeding six and a half millions of tons, avoirdupois, of two thousand pounds each, in weight—a structure which occupied, as

Herodotus informs us, a hundred thousand men no less than twenty years in building. It is a little remarkable, also, that Mr. Taylor, in the same work in which he ascribes the building of the pyramid to Noah and his descendants, and especially to Joktan and his thirteen brothers, quotes no less than five times the great work of Col. Howard Vyse, published in 1840, in which it is shown from inscriptions found in the monument itself, in the cavities called construction-chambers, discovered by him—cavities closed up by the builders and intended never to be visited—that the tradition which ascribes the construction of this stupendous monument of folly to King Khufu (otherwise Suphis or Cheops), of the fourth of the dynasties of Manetho, is correct.

The metrological theory of the pyramid has been accepted on faith by many who have not examined it themselves, but who have been carried away by the apparent ardor of conviction, and very real and fiery dogmatism, of its devotees. It has been made an article of faith by the "Institute for Preserving and Perfecting Weights and Measures," above mentioned; which Institute places at the head of its circulars the figure of the pyramid, over which is a miniature pyramid, resplendently radiant, and symbolical of the light which this structure was designed, according to the hypothesis, to shed upon the world. It is a part of the theory that the metrological system embodied in the pyramid is almost exactly identical, as to all three of the units of length, capacity and weight, with that which is at present in use among ourselves, and which, having been received from our Anglo-Saxon forefathers, has been somehow miraculously transmitted to us through them, from the time of its founders. The doctrine of the pyramid has become, therefore, something more than a speculative hypothesis: it has become, to borrow an expression from Mr. Proctor, nothing less than "a religion." The advocates of a real improvement of the world's systems of weights and measures cannot, therefore, afford to let this singular theory pass wholly unnoticed. If the issue concerned opinions only, they might be content to let it run its course, in the assured certainty that it would, in due time, die a natural death. Its practical bearing, however, so far as the minds of men are affected by it, is pernicious, inasmuch as it seriously obstructs measures of the highest importance to the amelioration of the condition of man in society, and to the facilitation not only of commercial exchanges, but of intelligent intercourse between nations.

It is on this account that I propose, in the present paper, and in one which I hope to present to the society hereafter, to examine this theory, which may, I suppose, with propriety, be called the Theory of *the Divine Legation of the Great Pyramid.*

I shall endeavor first to state, with some attention to detail, what this theory is. I shall then inquire what are the ascertained facts alleged in its support, and shall seek finally to examine how far these facts justify the deductions which have been made from them by the preachers of the pyramid faith.

The doctrine in question then affirms, first, that the external dimensions of the pyramid have been determined by means of a unit of linear measure which is one ten-millionth part of the polar radius of the earth; and that this unit is identical in length with the cubit intended in the instructions given to Moses for the construction of the ark of the covenant and of the tabernacle and its furniture, as recorded in the twenty-fifth chapter of Exodus. It is also assumed that the twenty-fifth part of this cubit exceeds one British inch by the one-thousandth part only; that is, by a difference equal to the thickness of an ordinary spider line. It is inferred, therefore, that this is the original value of the British inch, which, during the past four thousand years, has degenerated by one one-thousandth part. Accordingly, for the sake of distinction, the twenty-fifth part of this cubit (called, from its supposed origin, the sacred cubit) is spoken of as *the pyramid inch.* It follows that the pyramid inch is one two-hundred-and-fifty-millionth part of the earth's polar radius, or one five-hundred-millionth part of the earth's polar axis.

The next proposition of this surprising creed is, that the linear measure of one side of the pyramid, at its base, contains this sacred unit of measure as many times as there are days in the year, including the fraction of a day beyond the three hundred and sixty-five; that is, that the base measure equals 25×365.2422; this last number expressing in days the length of the tropical year. There was some hesitancy for a time as to whether the sidereal year of 366.2596 days should not be taken, as measures may be found among the different authorities which will easily accommodate themselves to either; but the tropical year has been finally accepted; and it is at present orthodox to believe in it.

The third proposition is, that the height of the pyramid (in its original and perfect condition) when multiplied by the ninth power of *ten*, expresses the distance of the sun from the earth with an exactness which puts to shame all determinations from transits of Venus, oppositions of Mars, perturbations of the moon, or any other method depending on merely human science.

We are next informed that the daily motion of the earth in its orbit is expressed " in the round decimal number of 100,-000,000,000 pyramid inches." It seems to be a consequence resulting from the superhuman character of the sacred cubit, that a variety of great natural dimensions measured by it are expressible in "round decimal numbers."

In order to understand the propositions which are to follow, reference must be made to a diagram showing the disposition of the passages and open spaces on the interior of the pyramid, so far as they have been discovered, with their relations to each other.

The figure shows a vertical section through the pyramid, in the plane of the axes of its interior passages. The strong line bounding the figure shows the exterior surface of the structure in its present injured condition. The fainter line without marks the finished surface, as it existed before the covering of compact and polished Mokattam limestone had been torn away. The descending entrance is marked A. The irregular passage, marked B, is the forced entrance made by the Caliph Al Mamoun, about the year 820 A.D. This does not intersect the regular passage, A, though it passes it at a distance of about twenty feet to the west and meets the ascending passage, marked D, farther on. E is a horizontal passage leading to F, the so-called queen's chamber. G, G is the grand gallery, H is the ante-chamber, K the king's chamber, with I, the sarcophagus, otherwise called the coffer, within it. At L are the cavities in the masonry over the king's chamber, supposed to have been left to prevent the crushing in of the ceiling of that chamber by the weight of the superincumbent mass. M and N are the passages supposed to have been intended for ventilation. O is the subterranean chamber, unfinished. P is the irregular passage called the *well*, through which the workmen are presumed to have effected their retreat, after effectu-

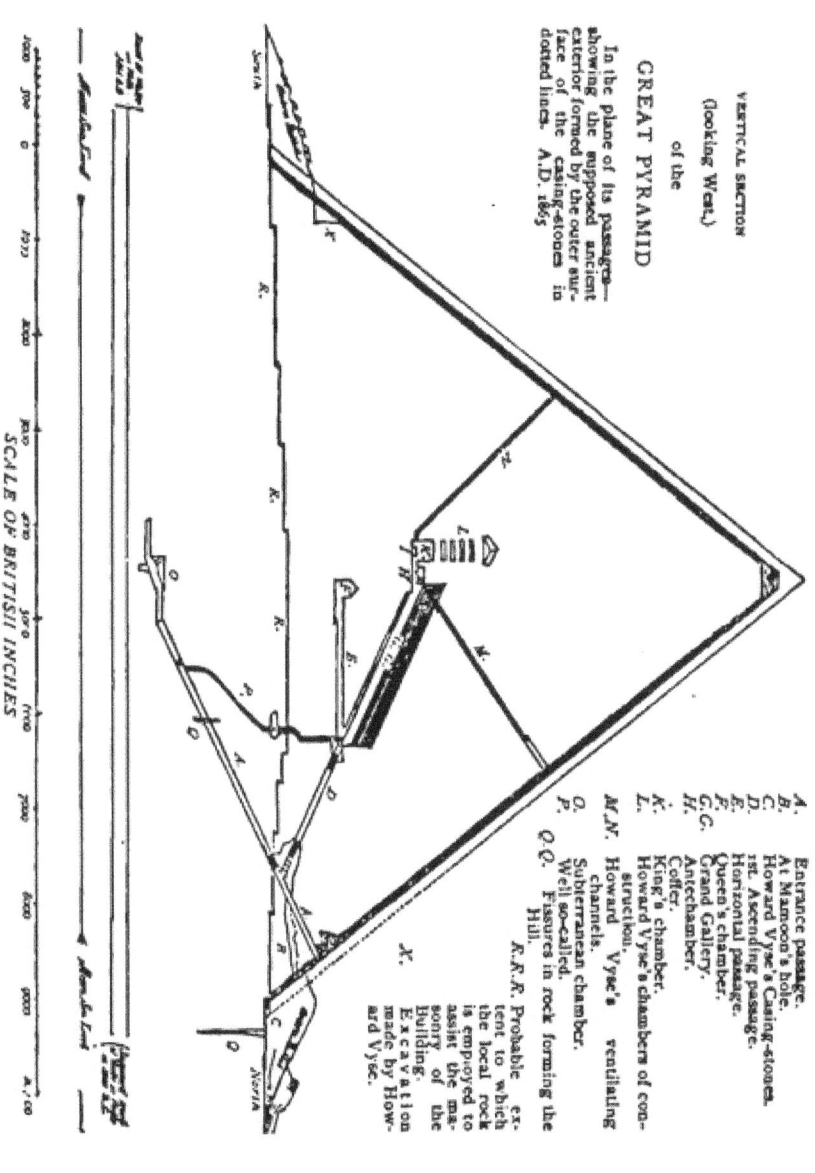

ally plugging up with granite blocks, the lower end of the ascending passage D, at the point where Al Mamoun's forced passage meets it. Q, Q are natural fissures in the rock on which the pyramid is founded. R, R, R are terraces cut in the rock in preparing for the building. X is a cut made in the south side of the pyramid by Col. Howard Vyse, in 1837. This is not a place to give a description of this remarkable monument. Those who wish to inform themselves more particularly about it, are referred to the great work of Col. Howard Vyse published in London in 1840, and to Prof. Piazzi Smyth's "Life and Work at the Great Pyramid," Edinburgh, 1867. The object of the introduction of this illustration (borrowed from the work last named) is simply to make the references in the present article to the different parts of the structure spoken of, intelligible.

Referring to this diagram, we proceed with the doctrine of the pyramid. In the further unfolding of this doctrine, it is next to be stated that the lengths of the principal of the passages here shown are affirmed to have been determined with reference to three of the most important events in the history of the human race, viz., the dispersion of mankind at Babel, the Exodus of the Israelites from Egypt, and the birth and crucifixion of Jesus Christ. The passages are assumed to be measures of the lapse of time, each inch of length being representative of a year. Thus, from the beginning of the descending entrance passage down to the point at which this is intersected by the passage ascending, we have the interval between the dispersion and the Exodus; from the intersection just named to the beginning of the grand gallery, we have the duration of the Jewish dispensation ending with the birth of Christ; from this point measured horizontally to the mouth of a nearly vertical but irregularly descending passage called the *well*, is represented the duration of the life of the Saviour, the thirty-six months of his active ministry being more particularly symbolized by significant accompanying peculiarities of construction. At the point marked as representing the birth of Christ, the ascending passage, previously low and narrow, not exceeding about fifty-three inches in vertical height by forty-one and a half in breadth, suddenly expands to magnificent dimensions symbolizing the glorious freedom of the Christian dispensation, as contrasted with the previous narrowness and severity of the rule of the law. This gallery ends at its southern and highest extremity in a wall which leans northwardly by an inclination of not less than a degree. What the pyramid religionists understand by this inclination may be gathered from the following remark concerning it taken from the new and enlarged edition of the work of Prof. Piazzi Smyth, entitled "Our Inheritance in the Great Pyramid," published in 1874. "The Bible," says Prof. Smyth, "fully studied, shows that he [Christ] intended that first dispensation to last only for a time; a time, too, which may terminate much sooner than most men expect, and shown by the southern wall *impending*." As the length of the grand gallery, measured from the point marking the birth of Christ to the south inclining wall, is on one side of it 1882.6 inches in length, and on the other 1883, or in the mean, 1882.8 [Smyth's "Life and Work of the Great Pyramid," ii. pp. 76, 77], it is evident that the impending crisis, whatever it may be, is due in this present year, and that the point of time at which it was to manifest itself is already past.

The article of the pyramid faith next to be mentioned, is that the object found in the king's chamber, having the form and general appearance of a sarcophagus, and which, until the publication of John Taylor's work, had always been regarded as such, is not a sarcophagus at all, but a measure of capacity, equal to four British "*quarters*" of eight bushels each. The name *quarter* continues to be in use in England, but there is no grain measure in use there of which this is a quarter in capacity. The name is assumed to be a survival from some period of antiquity in which the recognized unit was equal in capacity to this pyramid coffer. This object, called a coffer by the pyramidists, and a sarcophagus by the scoffers, has not, it is true, in its present condition, the capacity asserted. One side of it has been cut down nearly an inch and three-quarters, and the other three sides have been cut down on the interior to the same depth, leaving a depressed horizontal ledge evidently designed to support a lid. The inner surfaces of the cut on these three sides lean inward, or are shown by parts remaining to *have* leaned inward when perfect, so as to form a dovetail, plainly designed in this, as in other sarcophagi, to prevent the lid, when in place, from being lifted. No lid, however, has been seen by writers within the last three centuries; and it seems to be matter of doubt with true believers whether there ever was a lid. Some, apparently, incline to think that the cutting down and preparation *as if* to receive a lid, is a work of profane intruders, executed long after the completion and sealing up of the pyramid; but no doubt is entertained at all that the ruling purpose for which the coffer was constructed was to express a capacity such as *would* now belong to the vessel if restored to the form of a regular box, by replacing on every side the parts which have been cut away. There are some curious relations of number or volume said to exist between the exterior and interior dimensions of this coffer, and also between the coffer itself and the apartment in which it is situated; but these, if real, though they may illustrate a certain capricious ingenuity on the part of the designer, have nothing to do with the character of the box as a standard of capacity.

The geographical position of the monument is also an article of the pyramid faith. It stands very nearly on the thirtieth parallel of north latitude. The design of the builder was evidently to place it exactly on that parallel; but the rocky eminence on which it is founded fell off a little more than a minute of space too soon, and its actual latitude is 29° 58′ 51″. The motive inducing the choice of this latitude, according to the Pyramid religion, was that its interior temperature might correspond to the mean temperature of the entire inhabited world, which is assumed to be that belonging to the climate of 30° north latitude. Its longitude, moreover, was not matter of indifference. Its builders, according to Prof. Piazzi Smyth, were of a race not native to the country, who came into it from the East, for no other purpose but to erect this prophetic monument, and who retired from it toward the East again after their mission had been fulfilled. That their mission was divine is further inferred from the fact that they never built any architectural structure comparable to this, either in Egypt or outside of it, or even any other of importance at all, either before their intrusion into the Nile Valley or after they had left it. The inference is that Egypt was, by some geographical necessity, the country in which this mission had to be accomplished. The nature of this necessity, as it is regarded by the faithful, may be inferred from the following extract taken from Prof. Smyth's work above cited, "Our Inheritance in the Great Pyramid," p. 67. "Proceeding along the globe due north and south of the Great Pyramid, it has been found by a good physical geographer as well as engineer, William Petrie, that there is more earth and less sea in that meridian than in any other meridian all the world round, causing, therefore, the Great Pyramid's meridian to be just as essentially marked by nature across the world as a prime meridian for all nations measuring their longitude from, as it is more minutely marked by art and man's work for the land of Egypt alone. Again," he continues, "taking the distribution of land and sea in parallels of latitude, there is more land surface in the Great Pyramid's parallel of latitude than in any other. And, finally," he concludes, "on carefully summing up all the dry land habitable by man all the wide world over, the center of the whole falls within the Great Pyramid's territory of Lower Egypt." We are constrained, therefore, to believe it to have been a part of the divine purpose in locating the Pyramid, to make known to man the exact position of the geographical center of the habitable world. And accordingly it is not surprising that Prof. Piazzi Smyth is now a declared advocate of the adoption of the meridian of the Great Pyramid, as the prime meridian from which all the nations of the earth should reckon their longitudes.

In regard to temperature, Prof. Smyth says of the 30th parallel: "That 30° zone represents the climatic conditions of a larger part of the earth than any other possible zone; and being also the parallel which has in either hemisphere an equal amount of surface between it and the pole on one side, and between it and the equator on the other, it cannot help being somewhere very near to a golden mean between the far too hot tropics and the far too cold arctic and antarctic circles; while at the same time it receives *more* sunshine, more vivifying influence to man than any other latitude by reason of its paucity of clouds combined with the high solar altitude."

The mean annual temperature of the Egyptian plain of latitude 30° he admits to be a little above the mean of that latitude generally; but this, he says, is corrected by the hypsometrical elevation of 4,297 inches of the king's chamber above the sea level. This true mean temperature he places at 68° F. = 20° C., or one-fifth exactly of the distance on the thermometric scale between freezing and boiling water; and this is the temperature which the inner chambers of the pyramid, sheltered by the vast thickness of the rock around and above them, were designed to maintain.

The pyramid was further intended, according to the modern

expounders of its teachings, to instruct men as to the mean specific gravity of the earth. It appears from a comparison of the various results of modern scientific investigations of the earth's density, that the specific gravity of the entire planet is probably 5.7. But when the cubic contents of the coffer (the pyramid unit of capacity) are divided by the tenth part of the cube of fifty inches (two sacred cubits), which is 12,500, the result is exactly 5.7. The logic of the argument is not quite clear, but the arithmetic is unimpeachable.

In connection with specific gravity, another curious proposition is stated by the disciples of the pyramid faith, which is that the total weight or mass of the pyramid, estimated in pyramid tons (a pyramid ton equals 2,500 lbs. avoirdupois) bears the round decimal ratio to the total mass of the earth of one to one thousand million of millions—1 : 1,000,000,000,-000,000. In calculating the pyramid's mass, due account is taken of the cavities in the interior, of the different kinds of stone employed in its construction and the quantities of each, with their separate specific gravities. In the computation of the earth's mass, also, due account is taken of the spheroidal figure, and of the mass of the land above the mean sea level. No exception can be taken to the methods employed in these calculations; but the result, though curious, seems to be without any practical importance, and certainly shows no evidence of design.

It is a further article of the pyramid faith that, by the peculiarities of its construction, this monument marks the date of its own erection. It is truly oriented to the cardinal points of the compass, and a vertical plane through the axis of its inclined entrance chamber is very closely near to the true meridian. This passage also inclines downward at an angle which, from a mean of many measurements, Professor Smyth gives as 26° 27'. From below upward it therefore rises at the same angle. Its situation in the meridian and this inclination directed so nearly to the pole (which in this latitude has, of course, an elevation of 30°) has suggested naturally to many observers the idea that it was intended for the observation of what we call the pole star. But as this star is only about one degree and a third distant from the pole, while the axis of the passage is directed to a point 3° 33' below the pole, it is evident that, to a person deep down in the passage, our present pole star cannot be visible at any time during its daily revolution. Since, however, owing to the precession of the equinoxes, the pole of the earth has a retrograde azimuthal motion on the ecliptic amounting to about 1° 23' 40" per century, it is certain in the course of between twenty-five and twenty-six thousand years to encounter or pass near every star in the northern heavens having a celestial latitude of about 66½°. Now it is a rather singular fact that, in the entire small circle of the heavens thus described, there is not a single star fulfilling this condition, and sufficiently conspicuous to attract attention and to be probably treated as a pole star, except one known by the modern name of Alpha Draconis. It is, indeed, true that there is another of great brilliancy, viz., Alpha Lyræ, a star of the first magnitude, which, at one point of the great precessional year, approaches the pole within a little less than five degrees, and so might answer, though rather imperfectly, the purposes of a pole star; but more than nineteen thousand eight hundred years have passed since Alpha Lyræ occupied this position, and even then it was out of the field of vision of the pyramid passage. Alpha Draconis, however, about four thousand years ago, was within 3° 42' of the pole, and, at its lower culmination, could be seen by an observer anywhere in the entrance passage of the pyramid. But it is further held by orthodox pyramidists, that the *ascending* passage and the grand gallery were not without their astronomical use as well as the entrance passage, although they could only have been astronomically useful during the progress of the building and before they were covered up by the advancing masonry. The Pleiades were nearly opposite in right ascension to Alpha Draconis, at the time when the latter was the pole star; and Eta Tauri, the distinctive star of that cluster, passed the upper meridian almost isochronously with the passage of Alpha Draconis over the lower. The Pleiades were at that time on the equinoctial colure, or at the right ascension 0°, and, as Prof. Smyth remarks, "this group of stars has been more bound up with human history, hopes and feelings, than any other throughout the sky." As the builders of the pyramid are presumed to have designed to mark by it the commencement of the great precessional year, they would naturally begin that year when the Pleiades and the equinoctial point were in the same meridian. The exact date of beginning was that particular day which, at the period named, must have come at some time during the year, when Eta Tauri was passing the meridian at midnight, while Alpha Draconis was in view through the entrance passage of the pyramid on the meridian below. Now there were two dates at which Alpha Draconis could have this particular distance from the pole—one at 2170 B.C., and the other at 3440 B.C. But it was only at the first of these dates that the two stars in question were thus opposed to each other in right ascension. The former, therefore, was the date at which the pyramid observers could determine the beginning of the great precessional year by observation through its chambers and passages, while the work was still in progress; and this it is which fixes the date of this foundation at 2170 B.C. The date of the foundation is said also to be recorded more directly and more distinctly by a mark in the descending entrance passage. It has been stated that the beginning of the Grand Gallery is regarded as denoting the date of the birth of Jesus Christ. From this point, 1542 inches measured backward brings us to the intersection of the passages, and 628.5 inches measured backward from this intersection lead to two strongly ruled lines directly opposite each other, on the sides of the entrance passage; which further distance added to the previous 1542 gives 2170.5, and brings us to the same point of time B.C. which has been deduced as above from the appulse of the star Alpha Draconis to the pole.

Many of the imputed properties of the pyramid, or of its chambers, passages and minuter parts, are here passed without notice, because though, by force of a great deal of arithmetical ingenuity, they are made to show some unexpected —perhaps accidental, perhaps intentional—relations, they have no important bearing on the question of divine guidance or inspiration, and can at most only serve to betoken, on the part of the builders, some acquaintance with scientific truths of which we have supposed the people of so distant a generation to be ignorant. Thus, in the proportions of parts and the assignment of dimensions we are told that the pyramid has a pervading character throughout of what is called *fiveness*, of which the first illustration is found in the fact that it has five solid angles, and five sides (including the base). But though fiveness is the ruling arithmetical character, other numbers share in this honorable distinction. Thus Prof. Smyth remarks that "though in a lesser degree than five, *four* may be considered a pyramid marked-out number; because four is the number of sides of the square base, and four is the number of the triangular faces and flanks." "*Three* and *seven*," he goes on to say, "have likewise been suggested by William Petrie as numbers connected with the Great Pyramid. Though, too, at present these numbers are only to be dimly seen in a rather abstruse manner (notwithstanding that they are general and universal to the whole surface), yet they have the discriminating merit of belonging to the Great Pyramid only, of all the pyramids of Egypt and the world." ["Antiquity of Intellectual Man," p. 200.] Since *two* and *eight* may be considered as implied in *four*, since six is implied in *two* and *three*, and since nine is the square of *three*, it would seem to be the singular privilege of this remarkable structure to derive a peculiar character from every one of the nine digits.

But the property of the Great Pyramid which is put forward first of all by Mr. John Taylor and Prof. Piazzi Smyth as offering perhaps the most indisputable evidence of the preternatural knowledge and divine guidance of the builders, is that it is what is called for the sake of brevity a π Pyramid. By this is meant that its vertical height has to the perimeter of the base the ratio borne by the radius of a circle to its circumference: a ratio expressed by $1 : 2\pi$; π having the well-known value of 3.14159. This is a property which is independent of the magnitude of the structure, and of which the presence or absence can be ascertained with certainty, if it is possible to determine its angles. It rests, therefore, upon a very different foundation from the speculations which depend on measurements of the base dimensions, concerning which there is at present no certainty whatever.

The foregoing propositions embrace all the essential doctrines of the pyramid religion. Of the thousand marvelous details of curious numerical relations which have been discovered or imagined to exist between the various dimensions of the chambers, the ante-chamber, the grand gallery and the mysterious coffer, no account has been taken, because, whether true or otherwise, they are not above a moderate human intelligence, and have nothing to do with the question of inspiration.

I now propose to look into the facts upon the basis of which this extraordinary hypothesis has been erected. And, in the first place, as to the unit of linear measure which is asserted to possess at once these three characteristics. 1. It is the one ten-millionth part of the earth's polar radius, or one twenty-millionth part of the earth's polar axis. 2. It is in length exactly equal to 25.025 British inches. 3. It is identical with the sacred cubit of the Israelites. Unfortunately for the proposition under consideration, it is hopelessly weak in each of its three legs. There is no evidence, in the first place, that the builders of the pyramid used, or intended to use, any such unit of measure as the ten-millionth part of the earth's polar radius. History furnishes no testimony to this fact. Tradition is equally silent with regard to it. The builders themselves have left no record of it, in the form of inscription or otherwise. The proposition is a mere guess of Prof. Piazzi Smyth, to which he appears to have been led by a train of thought which he himself describes as follows,—the statement is condensed from his work above cited "*Our Inheritance*," &c., pp. 28, 29. Though his own words are not cited in full, no injustice to the sense is done in the abridgment. He asks himself what numbers in a π pyramid will express the ratio of linear height to twice base-breadth more simply than π itself with its inconvenient decimal; and he finds such numbers in the ratio of 116½ : 366. This number 366 appears to him suggestive. It is the nearest even number of days in a year; "or more precisely," he remarks, " of solar days in a mean tropical year." Now it appears that the side of the base of the pyramid, measured between the sockets which mark the places of its original corner stones (now wanting) both by the French scientific commission in 1799, and by Col. Howard Vyse in 1837, when it comes to be divided into 366 parts, seems to give to each of them a length approaching nearly to one ten-millionth of the earth's semi-axis of rotation. Equivalent, therefore, if further and independently proved, to the architect having laid out the size of the Great Pyramid with a measuring rod twenty-five inches long in his hand, and in his head the number of days and parts of a day in a year; coupled with the intention to represent that number of days in terms of that rod on each base-side of the building. This is really the whole of the argument.

The suggested division having been made, gives for the French measurement a quotient of 25.037, and for that of Col. Vyse, 25.049. Both are too large for the purpose, and both become still larger, if, instead of dividing by 366, we use as a divisor the exact length of the tropical year, viz., 365.2422, which will give us, in the first case, 25.0886, and in the second,

25.102. The "further and independent proof" necessary was therefore looked for in measurements of the pyramid by other persons, from which a more satisfactory quotient could be derived; the quotient wanted being the ten-millionth part in British inches of another quantity quite unknown, but guessed by Prof. Smyth to be equal to 250,250,000 British inches. The quotient wanted was therefore 25.025. The only measurements of the side of the pyramid's base, besides those just named, which can be esteemed of any value, were made by Messrs. Aiton and Inglis, two British civil engineers, in 1865, and by surveyors belonging to the Royal Ordnance corps of Great Britain, in 1869. For comparison, all four of these measurements are here presented in a group, reduced to inches of British measure:

MEASUREMENTS OF THE SIDE OF THE PYRAMID'S BASE.

British inches.
1. By the French academicians (north side, 1799)................9,163.440
2. Col. Howard Vyse and Perring (north side, 1837).............9,168
3. Aiton and Inglis (mean of 4 sides, 1865)......................9,110
4. Ordnance surveyors (mean of 4 sides, 1869)...................9,130

The exact mean of all these measures is 9,142.86. But this, divided by 365.2422, gives a quotient of 25.0323, which is too large; and divided by 25.025 gives 365.35, which makes the year too long. It may be objected that the deviations from the result desired are here so slight that it is something like hypercriticism to demur to them. This consideration would be worthy of attention if the question before us were one of imperfect human accuracy; but when we consider that the builders were working under the guidance of divine and infallible wisdom, we cannot be permitted to doubt that the dimensions of the structure, as it left their hands, were true to the minutest fraction. We are compelled, nevertheless, to admit that the modern measurements of this structure above given were made by fallible men. It is on this ground that Prof. Smyth is induced to guess, once more, that if a perfect measurement could be made it would be close to 9,140 inches [what is needed is 9,140.176045] for he remarks that "as there are *internal* evidences that none of these measures, not even the last, were accurate enough to be depended on to the third place of figures, all men are at this moment left by the last pyramid base side measures of modern times in this predicament, viz. :—the theoretical length of 9,140 inches, which would imply such almost unutterable wisdom, or such inconceivably happy accident, for that primeval time on the part of the designer of the Great Pyramid, is really found *among*, or as though it were *one of* the best results of modern measures." From which we are to understand that because the result desired is *not* among the best results of modern measures, therefore it *is* among them. For, as he continues, "The variations, therefore, first from 9,163 to 9,168, then to 9,110, and then to 9,130, must be merely the *plus* and *minus* errors of the modern measurers; or of men intending honestly to do well if they could, but erring involuntarily, sometimes to one side and sometimes to the other of exactitude."

In the discussions of pyramid questions there is a great deal of talk like this. The thing wanted is not found, but men would have found it if they had known how; it ought to be there, and therefore it is there.

One thing in regard to this base measure—a measure the correct ascertainment of which is absolutely vital to the pyramid religion—must have forcibly struck every reader of Prof. Smyth's voluminous works upon the Great Pyramid—it is that though he resided in 1865 for five months at the pyramid, living all this time in an ancient tomb within a stone's throw of the object of his study; and though, during this long period of time, he occupied himself day after day incessantly and most assiduously in the minutest examination of every square inch of the pyramid's surface, its chambers, and its passages; and though he measured, with microscopic accuracy, every facing stone of its interior in every part, including the dimensions, vertical, horizontal and diagonal, of all its cavities, and especially the famous coffer, of which he made a most protracted and wholly exhaustive examination; though, moreover, he prepared himself for this investigation by providing himself with instruments of almost fabulous accuracy, among which were rods divided to hundredths of an inch, and corrected to thousandths, and an altitude and azimuth instrument with circles by the first of British artificers; and though the number of his measurements amounts to thousands, and the record of them fills an entire volume of his "Life and Work at the Great Pyramid," yet after all this protracted and patient labor, he came away at last without measuring the base side of the pyramid himself. Yet it was during his residence on the spot that the British engineers Aiton and Inglis visited Gizeh for no other purpose than to make this very measurement—the only measurement they were instructed to make at all—it was under his very eyes that they executed the work, the least satisfactory to him of all that have ever been made, but in the prosecution of which they proceeded with a thoroughness of which there had been no former example; having laid bare, for the first time, not two only, as the French academicians had done, but all four of the corner sockets; and having measured not the single northern side only, to which former measurers had confined themselves, but all the four sides; when, if they had been careless, he was there to detect their inefficiency; if they had been unskillful, he could not have failed to expose and denounce their incompetency; yet the result brought out by them in his own very presence gives, when tested for the value of the measuring unit, on the assumed sacred theory, the unsatisfactory result of 24.97 British inches. Why, when such an opportunity was afforded him as never before was presented to any measurer, when all the fiducial points of the base were exposed, when he was in possession of measuring instruments of an accuracy such as had never belonged to any previously applied to the purpose, and when the only reason for which he had visited the pyramid at all was to measure it, why did he not avail himself of these unexampled advantages to repeat immediately after these blundering engineers had completed their task, the work which they had executed so greatly to his disgust? He has never pretended to answer this question. I do not see how he can answer it.

It is true that he has represented this measure as a very difficult one to make, because of the huge talus of broken rock accumulated on each side except at the angles, in consequence of the ravages made in past centuries by the reckless and ignorant inhabitants of the country, who have stripped these majestic monuments of the earlier civilization of Egypt of their outer coverings for material to build the modern city of Cairo—accumulations which obstruct the view of one angle from another, and make measurement in a direct line between these points impossible. He has not told us what were the methods employed by the engineers whose measurements he witnessed; but we can suppose that they consisted in continuing the lateral lines of the structure parallel to each other to points where the rubbish heaps no longer intercepted the view, and then measured between the lines so produced. The only material error in the use of such a method would be in the possible deviation of the produced lines from true parallelism. But Prof. Smyth had a much better method open to him than that, if he had been disposed to use it. He is an astronomer by profession, and he had with him a splendid altitude and azimuth instrument, which he used to determine very exactly the orientation of the pyramid and the angular inclinations of its passages. If no two angles of the base were visible from each other, it was surely possible to find somewhere a point from which both could be seen. By planting the instrument at that point, and measuring the distances to it from each of the angles; and then with the instrument measuring the angle included between these lines, he would have had a triangle with two sides and the included angle known, from which the determination of the base would have been a simple operation. Or if any accidents of the ground should have made the direct measurement of long lines difficult, he could have measured a short base at a convenient distance from the pyramid, and by observing from both ends of this base he would have found the side desired by the same means by which he could determine the diameter of the moon. Such an operation, conducted with the skill of which Prof. Smyth is so accomplished a master, could not have failed to ascertain the quantity sought within less than an inch of possible error. The failure to apply this method, considering the relation of Prof. Smyth to the question to which so large a portion of the labor of his life has been devoted, cannot but be pronounced an omission entirely unpardonable.

It was an omission not only unpardonable, but also unaccountable, unless we adopt a supposition which, though it has a certain plausibility about it, I should be sorry to believe to be true, viz., that *he dared not do it*. I should soften, perhaps, this expression, and say rather that he had not the heart to do it. For he could not but feel that on this crucial test would depend the fate of a theory which he had cherished for years as the very apple of his eye; and in view of the result of the measurement of which he had just been himself a personal witness, and which he was so far from impeaching that he has since said, in words already quoted, that it was made by "men intending honestly to do well if they could," he could not but feel an apprehension that, if he were to do this thing, it would be his cruel fate with his own hand to topple into ruin the beautiful edifice he had been so long, so patiently and so laboriously toiling to create. If it was a weakness to shrink from such a hazard, it was a human weakness, and we must feel ourselves constrained to pardon, though we may regret.

Mr. Taylor has a different method of connecting the pyramid with the Earth's dimensions. It partakes of that curious and unexpected character which distinguishes so many of his discoveries, and justifies us in classing them among what may be called the surprises of the pyramid. Taking as the true base-measure Col. Vyse's determination in feet (not in inches, as above), viz., 764, and making of this a vulgar fraction, with unity for the numerator, he reduces this to a decimal and finds the result to be 0.00,130,890,052, which is, he says, treated as a whole number, the mean circumference of the Earth in feet. "That is," as he expresses it, "one English foot bears the same ratio to the side of the pyramid that the circumference of the Earth bears to one hundred thousand millions of English feet." It must be confessed that, if the builders really designed to incorporate into the structure a record of their knowledge of the great geodetic truth here brought to light, they could hardly have devised a more ingenious mode of covering it up. The foregoing number, viz., 130,890,052, gives the mean diameter of 41,663,600, which reduced by one six-hundredth part on supposition of a polar compression of one three-hundredth part, makes the polar diameter equal to 41,594,160.66 feet, or 499,129,928 inches. Mr. Taylor introduces this statement with the observation: "This may be deemed nothing more than a numerical coincidence; but when we recollect that this foot alone expresses this relation, and that the measure by which it is expressed may possibly have had its origin at this time, and may even have been *called into existence to denote this proportion*, it seems to be a peculiarity which deserves notice." Nothing could be more conclusive. There are, in fact, but two weak points in this argument: the first is that 764 is not the base measure of the pyramid, and the second that 130,890,052 is not the mean circumference of the Earth. Otherwise the reasoning is quite unexceptionable.

Incidentally deserving attention in this place is the discussion given by Mr. Taylor of the determination of the Earth's circumference by Eratosthenes—a determination presumed to have been founded on a direct measurement of an arc of the meridian extending from Syene to Alexandria, and which gave as a result 252,000 stadia, which, allowing eight stadia to the mile, as Mr. Taylor appears to do, gives 31,500 Roman miles for the circumference, which evidently indicates 10,000 miles as the diameter. The Roman mile being estimated at 4848.5 English feet, should thus give a circumference of 152,727,750 feet. Mr. Taylor adds: "But though Eratosthenes was wrong in assigning 31,500 instead of 27,000 Roman miles to the compass of the Earth, he was very nearly correct in stating the *proportion* which a sphere bears to its diameter, when he represents it by a ratio of 10,000 to 31,500. By his use of these figures, correctly if viewed in relation to the Great Pyramid, he shows that his knowledge was not derived from a new measure of the Earth, but from the proportions recorded in the Great Pyramid [in the fact, in short, that it is a π Pyramid]. Deducting *one-seventh* for his error, leaves 130,909,500 English feet for the circumference." That is to say, that because Eratosthenes made the circumference of the Earth to be 152,727,750 feet, or one-seventh too great, he would have made it, if he had not committed this blunder, 130,909,500 feet; so that his labors furnish the proof that this last is the true value. This reasoning addresses itself so directly to our intuitions that we are compelled to pronounce it irresistible.

Let us proceed to consider the second of the weak legs of our proposition, viz., that the unit of measure governing the exterior dimensions of the pyramid is exactly equal to 25,025 British inches. We have seen that this result cannot be obtained by applying the year-length theory to any of the direct measurements of the object itself. Shall we be more successful in regarding it as an aliquot part of the Earth's polar axis? The length of the polar axis of the Earth is a quantity which may with strict truth be pronounced to be, up to this time, absolutely unknown. It is a quantity not by any means easy to be ascertained, and which in all probability mankind will never exactly know. To measure it directly is obviously a physical impossibility. All that we can know about it is conjecture, dependent upon uncertain calculations of which the data are measurements made upon the surface of the planet. Such computations would, indeed, be sufficiently trustworthy, if the figure of the Earth were a regular geometrical solid; but the thing which the many measures thus far made of meridian arcs has taught us more emphatically than any other, is, that it has not that character at all. Till within recent years, the planet has been regarded as a regular oblate spheroid; on the ground first, that such is the necessary figure of equilibrium of a homogeneous plastic mass in rotation—and that the earth was once plastic cannot admit of a doubt; secondly, that, as a rule, the measured degrees of latitude on the Earth's surface are longer in the arctic than in the tropical regions; and thirdly, that the vibrations of the pendulum in different latitudes indicate that the center of gravity of the planet is more and more distant as we proceed from the higher latitudes to the lower. If the figure were geometrically perfect, the ascertainment of the length of its axis of rotation would be a very simple problem. All that would be necessary for its solution would be the measurement of two meridian arcs of a few degrees in length, in different latitudes—the more widely different the better. And it would be a matter of no moment whether these arcs were measured on the same meridian, or on meridians in longitudes widely different. After the earlier meridian measurements, the problem was attacked in full confidence of the truth of this hypothesis. The results, however, obtained from different comparisons proved to be discordant in the highest degree. Every two arcs combined gave a different value for the polar axis; the differences ranging from a few miles to sixty or seventy. It became evident that this method could not be successfully applied to meridians in different longitudes; but it was hoped that it would furnish more consistent results if confined to partial arcs of the same meridian. Even here, however, great anomalies immediately presented themselves. Col. Everest, the director of the great Indian meridian survey, in which an arc of twenty-one and a third degrees is divided into two sections, found that, when he compared the northern half of the northern section with the southern half of the same section, he found an ellipticity twice as great as when he compared the southern half of the northern section with the whole southern section; and that the values of the polar axis obtained from these comparisons differed nearly thirteen miles. In comparing arcs of different meridians (of which some fifteen or sixteen have been measured in different countries), this eminent geodesist obtained about seventy-seven different results. Gen. de Schubert, of St. Petersburgh, in 1859, in making similar comparisons, obtained twenty-one discordant results, the largest and smallest values of the polar axis so obtained differing nearly seventy miles. He necessarily concluded that the Earth is not a spheroid, but still continued to regard it as a regular geometrical solid—that is, an ellipsoid with three unequal axes instead of a spheroid with two. On this supposition, he made a new investigation, confining himself to the three long arcs of India, Russia, and France. The values for the axis deduced on this hypothesis from the Indian and the Russian arc differed only about fifteen hundred feet; but those derived from the Russian and the French were at variance to the extent of more than thirteen thousand feet. He accordingly rejected the French arc, and combining the results from the other two, assigning to the Russian arc double of the weight of the Indian, obtained a value for the axis of 41,707,467 feet,[1] or 500,489,604 inches. Sir John Herschel, considering this rejection unwarranted, made a similar combination of the three determinations, giving each a value proportioned to its length, and found the larger value of 41,708,734.9 feet, equal to 500,504,818.9, which comes pretty near the value desired by Prof. Smyth. Mr. Airy, Astronomer Royal, of England, made, in 1830, a combination of all the arcs which had been measured anywhere throughout the globe, and arrived at a result of 41,707,620 feet, or 500,491,440 inches. Later, Prof. Bessel, proceeding on a similar principle, made the axis 41,707,314 feet, or 500,487,768 inches. Col. A. R. Clarke, chief of the mathematical department of the British Ordnance Survey, published in 1866 the results of a very laborious investigation of this problem, conducted on a new principle, and gave as his final result, 41,707,536 feet, or 500,490,432 inches. Now, although some of these determinations approach very nearly to the desirable number of 500,500,000, yet only one of them comes up to it, and the mean of them all, which is 500,-

---

[1] Not having immediate access to Gen. de Schubert's paper, the numbers here given are taken from a reprint in Davies' Report on the Metric System, New York, 1871, of a Lecture by Sir John F. W. Herschel. The deduction, however, does not accord with the data there given, which are:

    Russian arc (25° 20') giving 41,711,019.2 feet.
    Indian arc (21° 21') " 41,712,534.2 "
    French arc (12° 22') " 41,697,496.4 "

Reduced to inches, these are:

    Russian arc gives 500,532,230.4
    Indian arc " 500,550,410.4
    French arc " 500,369,956.8

The combination of the Russian and Indian arcs, giving double weight to the former, gives 41,711,524.2 feet = 500,538,290.4 inches.

492,732.8, is more than seven thousand inches too small. While, therefore, we may admit that the approximation is sufficiently close to justify a not unreasonable hope on the part of the zealous pyramidist, that it may yet be closer, and certainly in the present state of the question to tantalize him to a most provoking degree, we must pronounce it to be still unproven that the governing unit of measure in the base of the Great Pyramid, even if it were, as it probably is not, an aliquot part of the Earth's polar radius, is a cubit of 25.025 British inches.

We come now to the third weak leg of our proposition—it is the assertion that the unit of measure in the Great Pyramid's base is the sacred cubit of the Hebrews. We know, traditionally, that there was a cubit in use among the Israelites which was called sacred, though Smith, in his Bible Dictionary, makes no mention of such a measure; but we do not know what that cubit was, and it may be set down as very certain that it was not equal to 25.025 British inches. What we know on the subject is mainly due to Sir Isaac Newton, a man who, in addition to having been the most illustrious of the investigators of exact science that England has ever produced, was probably the most profoundly learned in sacred archæology of the men of his time. In a dissertation on Cubits, and especially on the Sacred Cubit of the Hebrews, originally written in Latin, and translated and published in 1737, in the miscellaneous works of Prof. John Greaves of the University of Oxford, Sir Isaac has gathered all the evidence that is to be found bearing on the question; and after careful study, has reached the conclusion that the sacred cubit of Moses was not greater than 24.9389, nor less than 24.7262 British inches; and that its probable value was 24.7552. Prof. Smyth cites Sir Isaac's dissertation at length and with signal approval, but he differs from him in the conclusion reached, which he thinks should have been 25 inches with a slight addition. It should be remembered, nevertheless, that Sir Isaac was wholly unbiased by any preconceived views, and was simply and honestly in search of the truth. He had no pet theories to sustain, and no reputation at stake on the result of the inquiry. On the other hand, he was a man who for acuteness in sifting evidence, and soundness of judgment in forming conclusions, has probably never had a superior. All this can hardly be said with justice of the very ingenious writer who seeks to discredit him. But though there was no doubt a sacred cubit among the Israelites, so called probably because of its use in measuring sacred edifices and their furniture, all history and all tradition, even the Bible itself, may be challenged for evidence that there was ever a sacred cubit in any other sense—in the sense, for example, in which the pyramidists interpret the word—that is to say in the sense of a measure of which God himself defined the exact length and gave to them, as appears to be believed by this class of metrological fanatics, in the form of a material and visible prototype. The Jews of the present day have heard no such thing from their fathers; the Talmud is silent about it; and certainly there is no such assertion in the Bible, nor is there anything in that book which by any amount of straining will bear such an interpretation. The earliest mention of the cubit in the Bible is contained in the sixth chapter of Genesis, where particular instructions are given to Noah as to the dimensions to be given to the ark. The words are as follows: "Make thee an ark of gopher-wood; rooms shalt thou make in the ark, and thou shalt pitch it within and without with pitch. And this is the fashion which thou shalt make it of: The length of the ark shall be three hundred cubits, the breadth of it fifty cubits, and the height of it thirty cubits." And so on. We find here no such phrase as "The length of the ark shall be three hundred cubits, *according to the cubit which I give unto thee.*" There is no question of what a cubit is, or of how it came to be. It is mentioned as something which Noah knows well enough already, just as he knows gopher wood, the material of which he is to build the ark. There was certainly then at that time no divinely given cubit. Nor is there any reason to suppose that there was one later. In the instructions given to Moses for the ark of the covenant and he tabernacle with its furniture, cubits are spoken of just as before—that is to say, as measures already familiar to Moses. In the description of Solomon's temple in 1 Kings, Ch. VI., the word is used in the same way, as it is also in Esther, Ch. V., where the height of the gallows on which Haman is to be hanged is stated. Yet if it had been a part of the divine purpose to make the use of a particular measure of length a religious duty of his people, it is inconceivable that there should not be found somewhere in the sacred volume of the law, a definition of the thing they were to use, set down in terms too clear to be mistaken. In the eyes of the pyramidists, the Sabbath is not more sacred than the sacred cubit; yet the duty of observing the Sabbath is enjoined all through the Pentateuch with endless iteration, while of the sacred cubit we are not even told that such a thing exists. And this is true of a book in which rules are laid down with the minutest particularity for the government of men's conduct in matters of the most trivial importance. For example, "Thou shalt make thee fringes upon the four quarters of thy vesture." "Thou shalt not wear a garment of divers sorts, as of woolen and linen together." "When thou buildest a house, thou shalt make a battlement for the roof, that thou bring not blood upon thine house, if any man fall from thence." Deut. Ch. XXII. "Thou shalt not muzzle the ox that treadeth out the corn." "Thou shalt not have in thy bag divers weights, a great and a small." "Thou shalt not have in thine house divers measures, a great and a small." Ib. Chap. XXV.

When we find injunctions like this last, of which the Scriptures contain many, denouncing frauds accompanied by the use of false weights or false measures, how happens it that the sacredness of God-given weights and measures is nowhere appealed to, as constantly happens in denunciations of violations of the Sabbath? The answer is obvious. There never were any God-given weights and measures. All the weights and measures that were ever in use among men were equally of human origin, and in that sense equally profane.

I have said above that there is not a passage of Scripture which even by a strained construction can be interpreted to give evidence of the divine origin of the sacred cubit. There is, perhaps, one which at a first glance might seem to form an exception to this sweeping statement. It is found in Exodus, Chap. XXV, v. 9, where these words occur referring to the sanctuary or tabernacle: "According to all that I *shew thee*, after the pattern of the tabernacle, and the pattern of *all the instruments thereof*, even so shall ye make it." Here it is implied that visible patterns were shown to Moses for his guidance; and that these patterns embraced instruments which some may suppose to mean tools to be used in the work, among which very possibly, or it may be said probably, must have been a measure of length. But if we take the whole passage in its connection, this interpretation can hardly stand. For the patterns shown are those of the tabernacle and the instruments *thereof*—that is, the instruments belonging to it and to be used in it—and not instruments to be employed in making it. But whether this be so or not, if we suppose the cubit to have been among the "*instruments*," we must accept the logical consequence that, before Moses, there was no sacred cubit; a consequence nothing less than disastrous to the pretension that this same sacred cubit was used in laying out the pyramid; since, according even to the chronology of Prof. Smyth, the pyramid was built at least a thousand years before the Exodus, and, according to that of Bunsen and Brugsch more than sixteen hundred.

But though it is thus made morally certain that there never was any unit of length divinely imposed upon men for their use, and that the cubit governing the measurements of the pyramid's base was not a cubit of 25.025 British inches, nor the one ten-millionth part of the Earth's polar radius, yet there *was* a cubit of well-ascertained but very different length, which was unquestionably employed by the builders of the pyramid in every part of their work, external as well as internal. There is in the British Museum in London a double-cubit rule which was actually in use several thousand years ago at Karnak, and which, having been carelessly left by some workman in a closed cavity in the interior of a mass of masonry, was built up and preserved, until, by the dilapidation of centuries, its prison house fell to pieces, and it was restored once more to the light of day. This double-cubit measures just 41.472 British inches, which makes the single cubit equal to 20.736, a value already known as that of the royal cubit of Egypt; its length in the different buildings in which it has been used occasionally falling a little below that just given—a variation not uncommon and even inevitable in countries where a pretty sharp supervision and verification of the standards of measure and weight in the hands of the people is not kept up by governments.[1] This Karnak rule exactly measures the breadth of the entrance and first ascending passages in the pyramid. Five times its length measures the breadth of the king's chamber, and ten times its length measures the length of the same chamber. Fifty times its half-length—that is the single cubit,—measures the distance from the beginning of the entrance passage on the north (supposing the pyramid restored to its perfect shape) down to the intersection of the passages; seventy-one times

[1] In some instances the royal cubit appears to have fallen below 20.6 inches. It is commonly stated at 20.7 or a little below.

the same length measures the first ascending passage to the beginning of the Grand Gallery; ninety-one times the same measures the length of the Grand Gallery itself, and four times the same, its breadth; and, finally, taking the measurement of the base-side by Messrs. Aiton and Inglis as probably the best, four hundred and forty times the same cubit exactly measures the length of this important dimension on which the whole doctrine of the Divine Legation of the pyramid depends; leaving, therefore, no room to doubt that the same unit of measure was employed on the exterior just as certainly as it is admitted by the pyramidists themselves to have been employed within.

The article of the Pyramid faith which presents itself for examination next in order is the proposition that the height of the Pyramid is exactly one one thousand millionth part of the mean distance of the Earth from the Sun. Inasmuch as we do not know the exact mean distance of the Earth from the Sun, it is impossible to subject this statement to the test of a rigorous comparison; but inasmuch as the builders of the Pyramid knew in all probability a great deal less about the matter than we do, it is next to impossible that the proposition should be true. Supposing it, however, for the sake of argument, to *be* true, the fact may be accounted for on either of two hypotheses—it is true accidentally, or it is true intentionally. Against the first of these hypotheses, the probabilities are in the proportion of infinity to zero; and this alternative, moreover, would be rejected with scorn by the disciples of the Pyramid religion. But that the fact may be true *in the intention of the builders*, as asserted, we must assume for them a knowledge which we have no reason to suppose them to have possessed. This slight difficulty the true believers dispose of summarily, by taking it for granted that their human ignorance was illuminated by direct inspiration from on high. The orthodox doctrine on the subject, therefore, is that the true distance of the Sun was miraculously made known to the Pyramid architects, and therefore that the height of the structure itself was made not pretty nearly, but exactly, the one-thousand millionth part of that distance.

Now what are the facts on which this extraordinary assertion rests? Simply these: In 1867, Mr. William Petrie, having satisfied himself that the perimeter of the base of the pyramid " has been *proved* to symbolize a year, or the earth's annual revolution around the sun," and, further, " that the radius of that typical circle had also been shown to be the ancient vertical height of the Great Pyramid, the most important and unique line which can be drawn within the whole edifice," was moved by these weighty considerations to conclude that the same line "*must* represent also *the radius of the earth's mean orbit round the sun:* and in the proportion of $1 : 10^9$, or $1 : 1,000,000,000$: because, among other reasons, 10:9 is practically the shape of the Great Pyramid. For this building," he proceeds, "notwithstanding, or rather by virtue of, its angle at the *sides*, has practically and necessarily such another angle at the *corners*, that for every *ten* units its structure advances inward on the diagonal of the base, it practically rises upward, or *points to sunshine* by *nine*. Nine, too, out of the ten characteristic parts (viz., five angles and five sides) being the number of those parts which the sun shines on in such a shaped pyramid in such a latitude near the equator, out of a high sky." (*Our Inheritance in the Great Pyramid,* Edition of 1874, p. 48.)

This is the logic, and the whole of the logic, on the basis of which a fact is asserted which, to plain human reason and simple common sense, is so grotesquely improbable, that its possibility can only be defended by clothing it with the character of miracle. The true believers have not failed, accordingly, to be affected by a sort of painful misgiving lest this *a priori* argument should be found unsatisfactory to a skeptical world. They have therefore sought for a confirmation of their hypothesis in comparing the result furnished by it with those deduced from the most recent investigations of the solar parallax.

Since early in this century the mean distance of the sun has been generally taken to be about 95,000,000 miles. This value has been obtained from the parallax as computed by Encke at Altona, in 1822, with data derived from the transit of Venus of 1769; a parallax which he found to be 8".5776, giving for distance 95,454,000 British statute miles. In 1857, Prof. Airy proposed a new method for determining planetary distances, founded on displacements of Mars in right ascension, as observed morning and evening from a single station, when in opposition at its nearest approach to the earth. This method was applied in 1862, by observations made at Victoria, New South Wales, and by others made at the Royal Observatory, Greenwich, during the opposition of Mars in that year; and the results, as computed at Greenwich, gave a parallax of 8".932, and a distance of 91,551,000 miles. In the mean time,

Leverrier at Paris announced (in 1861) that in order to reconcile discrepancies in the theories of Venus, the Earth and Mars, it was necessary to assume a parallax approaching perhaps 8".95. From this is obtained a solar distance of 91,357,000 miles. Chambers (Astronomy, p. 3) assumes as a probable value of the parallax, 8".94, which gives 91,465,000 as the distance. On the other hand, Prof. Newcomb, in his Popular Astronomy says: "It would appear that the solar parallax must lie between pretty narrow limits, probably between 8".82 and 8".86; and that the distance of the sun in miles lies between 92,200,000 and 92,700,000 miles." Furthermore, Prof. Young in his recent book on the Sun, remarks: "It would seem that the solar parallax cannot differ much from 8".80, though it may be as much as 0".02 greater or smaller; this would correspond to a distance of 92,885,000 miles."

Besides the astronomical methods, of which there are others not here noticed, there is one of great scientific interest dependent on the velocity of light. The time required for a luminous impulse to reach the earth from the sun is known within about a second or less, so that if we can ascertain how far light travels in a single second, we are possessed of all the data necessary to secure a very close determination of the distance of the sun. Independent methods for the experimental solution of this problem were devised some years ago by Messrs. Fizeau and Foucault, of Paris; and one or the other of these methods has been repeated by Mr. Cornu in France, and by Lieut. Michelson of the U. S. Naval Academy at Annapolis. The results obtained by the experimenter last named, are regarded as very closely approaching to the exact truth. They give 299,900 kilometers as the velocity of light per second; and as light is 498 seconds in coming to us from the sun, we find the solar distance to be 149,350,000 kilometers, equal to 92,803,464 miles. This nearly corresponds to a parallax of 8".81 which would give a distance of 92,876,000 miles.

Now the distance of the Sun as worked out on the Pyramid theory is 91,837,000 miles. This is in the neighborhood of some of the astronomical determinations. It exceeds the lowest of them, and falls short of the highest. Prof. Smyth accordingly jumps, in this case as in many others in which a favorite quantity of his falls somewhere among several of the same class, directly to the conclusion that because his quantity is neither the smallest nor the largest, therefore it is the true one. But if we consider the judgments of astronomers as to these various determinations, we shall see that the inferior ones have no standing with them at all. Newcomb, our highest authority in this country upon physical astronomy, places the probable distance at about 92,500,000 miles, and Young puts it as high as 92,885,000; while the experiments on the velocity of light, which are esteemed to furnish the result most worthy of confidence, give a result almost identical with the estimate of Prof. Young. The Pyramid distance is, therefore, only about a million of miles too short; while, probably, the uncertainty which still attaches to scientific deductions is not so great as half a million.

But there is another consideration which is quite conclusive as to the question now under discussion. The pyramid is said to be, and appears to be really, a π pyramid. But in a π pyramid the height is equal to the perimeter of the base divided by 2π. In such a pyramid, when the base is given, the height is inalterably fixed, and cannot have a value assigned to it at the caprice of the constructor. Now it is a doctrine vital to the pyramid religion that the side of the base shall contain the sacred cubit of the Hebrews as many times exactly as there are days, integral and fractional, in the tropical year. The height must, therefore, be that which this supposition demands, and it can be neither more nor less. On the other hand, if the height had been arbitrarily fixed at one one-thousand millionth part of the earth's mean distance from the Sun, the side of the base must have had a value such as *this* hypothesis requires; and could not have been determined by the cubit and the number of days in the year. It exceeds all the bounds of credibility, it exceeds all the powers of credulity, to suppose that two such entirely independent and inconsistent schemes of construction should prove to be harmonious in their practical results. Such a coincidence is indeed physically possible, but the chance in favor of the possibility is less than one to some millions of infinites.

We have next to examine the pretension that the pyramid furnishes a measure, "in a round decimal number" of the daily progress of the earth in its orbit. Prof. Smyth introduces the announcement of this proposition in these magniloquent terms: "Already the Great Pyramid linear system—while still preserving its cubit reference by 10' to the Earth's polar axis—has yielded to the further researches of William Petrie the knowledge of a far grander reference yet in nature, and of a more comprehensive kind in science; but expressed in similarly round and even decimal repetitions of Pyramid numbers, and of Pyramid units of linear measure." (*Antiquity of Intellectual Man*, 1868, p. 258). Then, after drawing on our imaginations to conceive the terrific force but smooth uniformity with which this mighty globe, with its various and diversified freight, sweeps on through the vast fields of space, he continues: " And therewith comes the practical question, What given length of such path is swept over by the earth in that special period or standard for the measurement of time (so admirably uniform in itself, and so intensely important in ruling the affairs of men) as the interval represented by the whole earth turning upon its polar axis and bringing a day of toil and a night of rest to all the wearied nations of mankind. The answer is (as given by Mr. Petrie) if you employ Pyramid *units* or inches of linear measure, you may tell off that mighty standard of space and force in a round decimal number, or by 10^7; *i.e.*, by 100,000,000,000 of Pyramid inches." Now what if it should appear that this wonderful discovery, announced with such a flourish of trumpets, is no new discovery at all ; but is simply the reproduction, with a little change of form, of the absurdity we have just now disposed of? If it is true that the mean distance of the Sun from the Earth is one thousand million times the height of the Pyramid, and if it is at the same time true that the side of the Pyramid's base is 25 Pyramid inches multiplied by the number of days in the year, then the mean distance traveled daily by the Earth in its orbit must necessarily be exactly one hundred thousand millions of Pyramid inches; but if neither of these preliminary suppositions is true, or if both of them are false, the conclusion must be necessarily false also. True or false, however, it is so directly dependent on the other propositions whose importance has already been so abundantly exploited and magnified by the disciples of the Pyramid faith, that it ought to have been regarded, even by them, as unworthy of a separate mention, instead of being heralded as it has been, as the grandest of all the properties yet brought to light in the miraculous structure of their worship.

The interdependence here asserted to exist between the propositions cited may thus be briefly shown. For the sake of conciseness we will employ symbols. Let h represent the height of the Pyramid; y, the numbers of days (integral and fractional) in the tropical year; r the mean radius of the Earth's orbit; and m the Earth's mean daily motion in its orbit.

Then $2\pi r$ is the circumference of the orbit, and the mean daily motion in the orbit is expressed by

$$m = \frac{2\pi r}{y} \quad (1)$$

But we have already been instructed that the radius r is equal to the height h multiplied by 10^9, or that

$$r = h \times 10^9 \quad (2)$$

Substitute this value of r for r itself in equation (1) and we have

$$m = \frac{2\pi h \times 10^9}{y} \quad (3)$$

But we have also been told that the side of the base of the pyramid is equal to 25 Pyramid inches (the sacred cubit) multiplied by the number of days (integral and fractional) in the tropical year; and as there are four equal sides, the entire perimeter must be, therefore, equal to $100\,y$. And as this perimeter, is equal to the circumference of a circle of which h is the radius, it follows that

$$2\pi h = 100\,y \quad (4)$$

Substitute now this value of $2\pi h$ for itself in equation (3) and we have

$$m = \frac{100y \times 10^9}{y} = 100 \times 10^9 = 10^{11}; \text{ Q. E. D.}$$

But, as we have shown that equation (2) cannot possibly be true, and that equation (4) is just as inadmissible, it is hardly necessary to add that the daily motion of the Earth in its orbit has not the remotest chance of being a " round and even decimal repetition of Pyramid units."

Of the pretension of the Pyramid theory which we are next to consider, viz., that which asserts that in the longitudinal dimensions of its passages we have a record (prophetic it must have been) of the most important epochs of human history, it is difficult to speak seriously. If we were dealing with periods of which authentic annals have come down to us, as of the capture of Constantinople or of the Declaration of American Independence, it would be easy to subject this pretension to an unimpeachable test. But of the three dates which are specified as distinctly indicated in this monument, viz., the dispersion of mankind at Babel, the Exodus of the Israelites from Egypt, and the birth of our Saviour, Jesus Christ; to which we may add a fourth—the date of the foundation of the Pyramid itself—there is not one which is not contested. Furthermore, while these dates are all unsettled as points in chronology, their asserted record in the structure is likewise uncertain; for the reason that, with the destruction by violence of the outer coating of the Pyramid, the initial point of reference has been removed, and can now only be reëstablished by a conjectural restoration.

That conjectural initial point, we are told, represents in chronology the dispersion of mankind at the confusion of tongues in the building of the tower of Babel. This event is placed by some chronologists at about one hundred years after the deluge, and by others as late as four hundred years after that catastrophe.

But the date of the deluge itself is one of the most uncertain in all archæology. Authorities differ in regard to it to the extent of more than a thousand years. According to the Masoretic Hebrew text of the Old Testament, the creation of the world took place 4161 years before the advent of Jesus Christ, and the deluge 1759 years later; that is in B.C. 2402. According to the Samaritan text, the creation was 4305 B.C., and the deluge 1708 A.M., which would fix this latter event at 2597 B.C. According to the Vatican Codex of the Septuagint, the numbers are 5270 for the Creation, and 2663 A.M. for the Deluge, carrying the drowning of the world back to 2607 B.C. And according the Alexandrian Code, the year of the creation was 5508 B.C., the deluge being 2669 A.M., as before, removing the great flood still farther back to 2845. Petavius, a very learned chronologist of the seventeenth century, fixes on 2327 B.C. as the year of the Deluge; Archbishop Usher assigns the same event to 2348 B.C.; Hales to 3155 B.C.; and Jackson to 3170 B.C. The authors of the great work entitled *L'Art de Vérifier les Dates des Faits Historiques*, say that Noah went forth from the ark in the year 3307 B.C. Recent chronologists, however, are by no means content with even the largest of these numbers. The Chevalier von Bunsen, for example, puts the creation of Adam as far back as 20,000 B.C. and the birth of Noah at about 10,000 B.C. John Taylor adopts very nearly the chronology of Archbishop Usher, making the year 2349 instead of 2348. The difference is slight; but when we are considering a record of years said to be palpably recorded in inches of solid masonry, it is necessary to be particular. Prof. Smyth, who gives the date of the deluge only by implication, in giving, as we shall presently see, that of the dispersion from Babel, makes it somewhere between 2600 B.C. and 3000 B.C.

It is the date of the dispersion, however, which specially interests us at present; since that is the date which, in the religion of the Pyramid, is the initial chronological point at the mouth of the entrance passage. John Taylor puts this at 2247 B.C., and Professor Smyth at 2528 B.C. There is a rather startling discordance noticeable here between the disciple and the master, which tends seriously to shake our faith in the Chronology of the Pyramid. We must leave it for them to reconcile it between themselves, and in the mean time turn our attention to the testimony of non-Pyramidistic archæology.

There are naturally as many different dates assigned by different archæologists to the epoch of the dispersion as to that of the deluge. A few only need be cited in illustration here. The confusion of tongues is identified in time with the year of the birth of Peleg, a descendant in the fifth generation from Noah; and, according to the Alexandrian Codex of the Septuagint, Peleg was born in 2698 B.C. Archbishop Usher makes the date 2247. The authors of *L'Art de vérifier les Dates*, the most elaborate chronological work hitherto published, carry it back as far as 2907 B.C. These few citations may serve to show that what Professor Smyth loftily calls "The Floor Roll of the World's Religious History" has not even an ascertained starting point.

The next point in this great " Floor Roll of Human History " is the date of the Exodus of the Israelites from Egypt. But here we meet with a discord among authorities no less bewildering than that which we have already encountered. The dates assigned by different chronologists to the event in question vary to the extent of nearly six hundred years. The work already cited, *L'Art de vérifier les Dates*, places it at 1865 B.C. Brugsch, Lepsius and Bunsen, however, from the more recent study of Egyptian History as revealed in the monuments, bring it down, the first to 1300 B.C., the second to 1312 B.C., and the third to somewhere between 1314 and 1320 B.C. Between these wide limits we have Usher, 1491 B.C.; Wilkinson, 1495 B.C.; Petavius, 1531 B.C.; Jackson, 1593 B.C.; the Septuagint, 1614 B.C.; Clinton, 1625 B.C.; and Hales, 1648 B.C. John Taylor does not give us a date for the Exodus, probably because the "Floor Roll of Human History" was a discovery of his school and not of himself. Nor does Professor Smyth give it with that exactitude which we have a right to expect of him in a matter of such moment. His statement of the date, and of the manner of finding it, is as follows: "Measuring along the passages backward from the north beginning of the Grand Gallery (the point assumed to mark the birth of our Saviour), you find the Exodus at either 1483 or 1542 B.C., and the dispersion of mankind at 2528 B.C. up at the beginning of the entrance passage." (*Our Inheritance in the Great Pyramid*, 1874, p. 390.) This duplication of dates for the Exodus comes from the fact that the first of the backward measurements given extends only to the roof of the entrance passage, while the second extends to the floor. The mean of these measurements, viz., 1512.5, presents a third value of the date, which we are presumably at liberty to choose. But no one of the three exactly corresponds to any of the determinations of the archæologists, though the first approximates that of Usher, and the second that of Petavius; and both of these, according to the most recent interpretations of Egyptian inscriptions, carry the event in question nearly two hundred years too far back. Brugsch has made it very clearly evident that the Pharaoh of the Exodus was Mineptah II., a monarch whose reign began in 1300 B.C., so that the Exodus itself must have been of some years later date. (*Brugsch's History of Egypt under the Pharaohs*, 1881, vol. 2, p. 133.) We are compelled to conclude, therefore, that the "Floor Roll of Human History" can no more be relied on for the second of the important dates which are said to mark it, than it can be for the first.

As to the third of these dates, that of the birth of our Saviour—all archæologists agree that it is erroneously placed in the chronology generally accepted in these later centuries. In "*L'Art de vérifier les Dates*," the *Annunciation* is said to have taken place in the month of March of the 747th year after the foundation of Rome; in the second year of the 193d

Olympiad; in the 39th of the reign of Augustus; in the 25th after the battle of Actium; and in the 35th after the elevation to power of Herod the Great. This places it nearly six years before the beginning of the Christian era as at present counted, and makes the epoch fall five years too late—a view now generally acquiesced in. Smith, in his Bible Dictionary shows us, however, that great diversity of opinion has prevailed on the subject. "For example," he remarks, "the birth of our Lord is placed in 1 B.C. by Pearson and Hug; in 2 B.C. by Scaliger; in 3 B.C. by Baronius, Calvisius, Süskind and Paulus; in 4 B.C. by Lamy, Bengel, Anger, Wieseler and Greswell; in 5 B.C. by Usher and Petavius; and in 7 B.C. by Ideler and Sanclemente. To this we may add the computation of Father Magnan, whose *Problema de Anno Nativitatis*, published in 1772, is cited by the authors of "*L'Art de vérifier les Dates*," and which places the nativity in B.C. 8. In the "Floor Roll of Human History," however, the epoch of the vulgar era is supposed to be correctly placed, and the beginning of the Grand Gallery marks the year 0.

But if the place of this epoch has been contested relatively to others—to the Olympiads, for instance, or to the A.U.C. of the Romans—still larger have been the differences of opinion, in referring it to its place in the great stream of time commencing at the creation. The authors of the elaborate work already quoted, on verifying dates, have brought together no fewer than one hundred and eight estimates by different chronologers of the place of the Incarnation in the world's history. Of these, the largest is that assumed in the Alphonsine Tables, edited A.D. 1782 by John Müller, otherwise called Regiomontanus, in which the birth of Christ is placed *Anno Mundi* 6984, and the smallest is that of L. Lippeman, Venice, 1554, which places the same event in A.M. 3616. The authors of the work referred to, themselves adopt the date A.M. 4963. A table of different opinions as to this matter made by Hales, embraces one hundred and twenty different estimates; and Mr. George R. Gliddon (*Types of Mankind*, 1854, *Supplement*, p. 658) says that this number could easily be extended to three hundred.

While all prehistoric archæology is in a state so utterly unsettled and uncertain, it is impossible to conceive an assumption more wild or unwarranted than that which asserts that we have here, in a monument constructed by human hands, a record and measure of the intervals separating the most important events in human history, laid down in exact inches of length more, probably, than sixty centuries ago, and certainly not less than a thousand years before the events themselves had taken place. Let it also be borne in mind that this strange myth is a mere guess; that not a shadow of evidence has been produced to show that any such childish purpose was ever in the minds of the constructors of this monument as is here imputed to them. If they had designed to build so curious a riddle into the structure, is it conceivable that they would have left behind them no key to its solution—and not only no key, but no intimation, no slightest hint, that there was really here a riddle to be solved? Supposing, on the other hand, no riddle intended, but an open and outspoken prophetic history, is it conceivable that they could have failed to tell, in some manner which posterity could not mistake, where the prophecy was to be found, and by what law of interpretation it was to be brought to light? *A priori* there was quite as much reason to suppose the height of the pyramid to be a measure of time, as the length of its passages; and as much reason to suppose the length of a passage to be a measure of the distance of the sun, as that the height of the pyramid should be so. In other words, there is no reason *a priori* that either of these things should be true; and therefore there is every reason to feel assured that, if the builders of the pyramid had had any lesson whatever to convey to coming centuries by the dimensions or by the proportions of parts of the structure they were engaged in rearing at so vast a cost of labor and time and wealth, they would have clearly and distinctly declared the fact in some form as enduring as the monument itself. Upon the exterior surface of the finished pyramid, there was once, according to Herodotus, a legible inscription; but the same authority informs us that it was nothing but a silly statement of the vast number of onions, radishes and cloves of garlic which had been consumed by the common workmen during the building. On its interior we know, from the testimony of all visitors, there has never been found in any place designed to be visited, a letter, a hieroglyphic or significant character of any kind; though the broad and smooth surfaces of its several chambers, its grand gallery and its marble finished passages, seem made for and to invite inscription. But they are all absolutely silent.

It is therefore an hypothesis utterly untenable to suppose

that this monument embodies any lesson of either science or history or religion, built into it by the benevolence of the earlier centuries for the benefit of the later; or that the builders had any other object in view in heaping up this monstrous pile of stone, but the accomplishment of some purpose immediately interesting to themselves.

But the fact that the pyramid fails to tell its own story is no more remarkable than this other fact that, in all Egypt, there has never been found on any monument, either contemporary with it or of later date, in the form of incised or painted inscription, or even in any papyrus roll, any, the slightest, allusion to this object whatever; still less any single word to throw light upon the purpose of its erection. On the other hand, since it belongs to a class all the rest of which are unquestionably sepulchral, it is impossible to resist the conviction that this was sepulchral also, even if it was not designed for sepulchral purposes exclusively.

To return once more to "The Floor Roll of Human History," it may admitted that the fact that there is a coincidence between dates of certain signal events in the world's history and certain linear measurements in an artificial structure, is one which at first view is well fitted to excite the imagination, if not even to compel the belief that the coincidence cannot have been unintentional. But this impression loses much of its force after it has been discovered that the dates in question are all of them uncertain, and some of them so to the extent of several centuries: so that they are in fact practically unknown. Moreover, even if the dates were all perfectly well ascertained the effect of the noticed coincidences would be greatly shaken if it should be shown that such correspondences are by no means unique; but that by the study of chronological tables they may easily be paralleled. Of such parallels the following may serve as illustrations: We have seen that Prof. Smyth places his earliest date, the confusion of tongues and the dispersion of mankind, at 2528 B.C. His intermediate point is determined by the intersection of the axis of the ascending passage with the roof or the axis or the floor of the entrance passage. The first intersection (which he assigns to the Exodus) would give a date of 1483 years B.C.; the second of 1512.5 B.C.; and the third of 1542 B.C. He has not distinctly pronounced in favor of any one of these dates, so that this point is left a little loose. The third great historical event presumed to be commemorated (foreshadowed, rather, from the builders' point of view) is the Advent.

Let us now take, on our own part, two dates of momentous interest, separated as nearly as possible by the same number of years which, according to Prof. Smyth, intervenes between the dispersion of mankind and the birth of our Saviour. We will choose for the earliest of these the foundation by King Solomon of the first temple at Jerusalem, an epoch commonly placed at 1013 B.C. For the other extreme we will select the great religious movement known as the Reformation, which commenced in 1517 with the protest of Luther against the sale of indulgences by Tetzel. These two dates united give a sum of 2530 exceeding the extreme limits of Prof. Smyth by only the insignificant difference of two years. The Advent itself forms the intermediate term, and takes the place of the Exodus in Prof. Smyth's series; being within five units of the point defined by the intersection of the axes of the two passages of the Pyramid, which would give 1512.5 instead of 1517. Have we not, then, as much reason to believe that the Pyramid builders intended to foreshadow here the building of the temple and the Reformation of Luther, as that they designed to predict the confusion of tongues and the Exodus from Egypt?

As another example, let us take the three epochs: the giving of the tables of the Decalogue at Mt. Sinai; the compilation of the Old Testament Canon by Ezra; and the preaching of the first crusade by Peter the Hermit by order of Pope Urban II. This last event took place in A.D. 1094, and 2528 years counted backward from that date carry us to 1434 years B.C., which falls about midway between the dates assigned to the Exodus by different archæologists. Ezra is said to have settled the canon of the scripture about 448 B.C., and between this date and 1094 A.D. is an interval of 1542 years, which corresponds to the date B.C. of Prof. Smyth's highest estimate for the Exodus. Thus we see that the Pyramid predicts to us very clearly not only the Exodus, but the reduction to systematic form of the inspired writings, and the commencement of the great series of religious wars waged for the recovery of the Holy Sepulchre.

Not to confine ourselves, however, to Hebrew or to religious archæology only, let us see if we cannot find coincidences equally striking elsewhere. In Græco-Roman history we have two signal events separated from one another by an interval of nearly 1500 years. The siege of Troy is an episode in the shadowy past, of which the date, like that of the dispersion of mankind, is uncertain between pretty large limits, and is generally ascribed, on conjectural grounds, to between 1100 and 1200 B.C. We will venture to take it at about 1075 B.C.; especially as, in all probability, the whole story is a myth. From this point of time onward to the downfall of the Eastern Empire, and the extinction of the last traces of Roman power, there is an interval of 2,528 years, which is exactly that required by Prof. Smyth's measurements from the mouth of the entrance passage onward to the beginning of the Grand Gallery. Also, between these two outside limits, we have the date of the battle of Actium, B.C. 30, which marks the beginning of the imperial form of government at Rome. This date added to 1453 gives a sum of 1483—exactly equal to the number of inches of the ascending passage of the pyramid, as measured back from the threshold of the Grand Gallery to the intersection with the roof of the entrance passage, which is one of the values of Prof. Smyth's later interval. Here, then, we have the Pyramid recording both the rise and the fall of the great Roman Empire.

Take again the following: The organization of the Roman State in its civil and religious institutions by Numa Pompilius dates at about 724 B.C. The accession to the imperial dignity of Constantine the Great took place in 306 A.D. Finally Napoleon Buonaparte was proclaimed Emperor of the French May 18, 1804. Between 724 B.C. and 1804 A.D. there is an interval of 2528 years exactly, and the accession of Constantine falls 1498 years earlier than that of Napoleon, which number is between the limits 1483 and 1542 of Prof. Smyth. Thus the Pyramid predicts the accession to power of the first Christian emperor and of the greatest conqueror of modern times.

There remains to be considered the enigma presented by the mysterious "ruled lines," which Prof. Smyth has found on opposite sides of the entrance passage, at a distance of 2170 inches as measured backward from the beginning of the Grand Gallery. These lines, according to him, fix the date of the foundation of the Pyramid; a point of time which, by subtracting the foregoing date from 2528, we find to correspond with the 358th year after the dispersion of mankind at Babel. Now there is something extremely suggestive about this number 358.

It is but a few units short of 365, the number of days in the tropical year. And as the original entrance mouth has long since disappeared, and can only be reëstablished by calculation or conjecture, the true place of that starting point may well be uncertain to the extent of seven or eight inches. The casing stones found by Col. Howard Vyse in 1837 at the foot of the northern slope were so large as to prove that the casing had been very thick; and it is quite possible that the mass of the pyramid beneath the casing may have been reduced when the casing itself was torn away, or later. This indeed, is quite possible in view of the enormous heaps of loose blocks which, not having been carried off by the destroyers, still encumber the foot of the monument on every side, as well as of the fact that the summit of the monument itself has been truncated to the extent of a twentieth part of its original height. One of the stones found in place by Col. Vyse measured more than eight feet along its base, at right angles to the Pyramid, and was no less than five feet in thickness. Prof. Smyth himself says that "the upper or northern end of the floor (of the entrance passage) is probably short by more than one hundred inches of the original surface of the Pyramid at that place." (*Life and Work at the Great Pyramid*, vol. 2, p. 37). He does not give us an account of how he established the true place of beginning, but he says that, in measuring backward from the entrance of the Grand Gallery we find "the dispersion of mankind in 2528 B.C. up at the beginning of the entrance passage." Now with a deficit to be supplied by doubtful calculation of, at any rate, "more than 100 inches," we may be justified in supposing that this number 2528 ought rather to be 2535, or perhaps 2535.2422, which would make the distance of Prof. Smyth's "ruled lines" downward from the entrance mouth just 365.2422 inches—that is to say, precisely as many inches as there are days (integral and fractional) in the tropical year. And there seems to be no good reason why the tropical year should not be recorded in inches here as well as in cubits in the side of the base. This theory is submitted as furnishing an explanation of the "ruled lines" riddle, quite as plausible as that which finds in it a record of the date of the Pyramid itself.

In this case, as before, we can arrive at a variety of results equally remarkable by adopting other historical epochs for the starting point. For instance, Solomon, the greatest king of Israel, was born, according to Hales, 1030 B.C. From this date, if we take 358 years, we have 672 B.C., which is the year in which Manasseh, the fourteenth king of Judah, after having been carried off into captivity by Asaridinus, King of Babylon, was set at liberty and permitted to return to Jerusalem.

If we start from the foundation of Rome in 753 B.C. and count onward in like manner 358 years again, we shall fall on the year 395 B.C., the year in which the city of Veii was captured by the Romans after a ten-years siege; or if we count 365 years instead of 358, we shall come to a much more important event—the capture and burning of Rome by Brennus and his Gauls.

The exodus of the Israelites from Egypt is put by Brugsch at 1300 B.C. Just 358 years later, viz., in 942 B.C., occurred the great battle in the Valley of Zephathah, in which Asa, the third king of Judah, defeated Zerah the Ethiopian and his army of a million of men (II. Chronicles xiv. 9) with an army greatly inferior.

The capture of Constantinople by Mahomet II, and the fall of the Eastern Empire, took place in 1453 A.D. If we count back from this date 358 years, we arrive at 1095 A.D., the year of the first Crusade.

The Diet of Worms assembled in 1545 A.D.; at 358 years earlier than that date, viz., 1187 A.D., Jerusalem was captured by the Saracen Sultan Saladin, after having been held by the Christians for nearly a century.

In 1850 A.D. California was admitted, as the thirty-first State, into the American Union. In 1492 A.D., 358 years before, America was discovered by Christopher Columbus.

These examples have been given merely for the purpose of showing how easy it is to find important dates in chronology to correspond to almost any series of two or three numbers taken at random; and therefore how little significance is to be attached to these measurements of the Pyramid's passages, which have been dignified by the name of "The Floor Roll of Human Religious History."

We will pass now to a topic as to which the importance in the Pyramid faith has been still more highly magnified, viz., the sarcophagus, or as it is more respectfully called, the *coffer* of the King's Chamber. This object seems to have concentrated upon itself a more earnest attention, and to have secured to itself a deeper interest, than anything else connected with the Pyramid. It appears to be looked upon by true believers with something of the same kind of veneration with which the Israelites were accustomed to regard the ark of the Covenant.

The character of this vessel, in its present condition, is too obvious to be mistaken. It differs in no respect from other sarcophagi, except that it is without ornament or inscription. As has been already stated, one of its sides has been cut down nearly two inches, and the other three sides have been undercut to the same level, evidently in order to allow a lid to be placed over it by sliding laterally. Moreover, as in other sarcophagi, there are holes, three in number, each about an inch in diameter, bored downward from the upper surface of the side which has been cut away, the purpose of which was to allow strong wooden pins, placed loosely in corresponding holes in the lid, to drop into them when the lid is pushed home to its place, so as to prevent removal by sliding, while the dovetail undercutting prevents removal by lifting. These peculiarities sufficiently indicate the purpose for which this object was constructed, and to simple common sense would seem to leave room for no further question in regard to its character. But simple common sense is not the quality for which our friends of the Pyramid persuasion are most remarkable. To them, this stone box had a more lofty design than that of receiving the body of any mortal man, however great or powerful. It is the visible embodiment of a divine message to men, prescribing to them the system of weights and measures by which they are bound to be governed in their dealings with one another. Primarily, it is a standard of capacity; but secondarily, it becomes a standard of weight likewise; and more indirectly still, a standard of length. Moreover, its capacity as a standard, must be understood of the capacity which belonged to it before it received those modifications which give it, at present, the appearance of a sarcophagus. In other words, in its original construction, all its sides were of equal height, and none of them were cut away in whole or in part. In that condition it constituted a measure of the unit of capacity from which all other measures were to be derived. The modification and mutilation of its form, which have thrown so much obscurity over its original design, are assumed to be outrages committed by sacrilegious hands in later but unascertained times. In corroboration of this view, it is remarked that the vessel, though prepared to receive a lid, has never had a lid since the time of its discovery in A.D. 820, by Al Mamoun; and that a sarcophagus without a lid is not a sarcophagus. The argument may be taken for what it is worth; but it seems to be attended with one or two slight difficulties, among which are the following:

1. Nobody knows what Al Mamoun found in the Pyramid, but all the world knows what he hoped to find, and that was treasure. If he found, as he probably did, the sarcophagus covered by a lid, he could hardly have failed to believe that within it lay concealed, not the body of the monarch only, but his jewels also. Nothing could be more natural than that he should seek to satisfy at once his curiosity and his cupidity by violating the sanctity of the tomb. But he could not remove the lid by either lifting or sliding. He therefore broke it, and the fragments of it have long since been carried away by the myriads of curious visitors who, during the more than one thousand years that have since elapsed, have successively penetrated into this mysterious vault.

2. Suppose that Al Mamoun found no lid; he did not cut down the coffer itself from its original form to the shape in which we find it at present. The undertaking would have been no slight one, for the material of the vessel is a compact syenitic granite, so tough that the knocks and bangings of hundreds of thousands of tourists, eager to secure splinters as mementos, have, after all, inflicted upon it no very serious damage, except at one corner. He could have had no motive for meddling with it, but every motive for getting away as fast as possible; for his men, worn out by their long and fruitless labor, were becoming disaffected to such a degree that he is said to have resorted to a ruse to content them, by secretly burying among the rubbish a treasure which they were at length permitted to discover and to share.

3. The alteration in the form of the coffer cannot have been made after the closing of the Pyramid by its builders, and before Al Mamoun's time ; for, though there is reason to believe that the entrance was discovered and that the interior had been visited at some early day, there is equal reason for supposing that such visitation was for destructive and not for constructive purposes.

4. The design of the builders was, unquestionably, to conceal the entrance, and the means they employed for this purpose were so effectual that, even after it had been found by the intruders just referred to, and closed by them a second time, it remained so difficult of detection that not the slightest sus-

picion of its existence was entertained by Al Mamoun, when he undertook and accomplished an entrance by violence. It is, moreover, not by any means certain that the King's Chamber was ever reached by any visitor before Al Mamoun, and if it was, it was hardly so more than once; so that little opportunity could have been found for making any changes there after the time of the builders. There is consequently the best reason for believing that the coffer, or sarcophagus, is at this day in the same condition in which it came from their hands, with the exception of the injuries it has suffered at the hands of modern tourists.

The difficulty of resisting the evidence that this object has existed in its present actual form from the beginning, is so great, that Prof. Piazzi Smyth actually concedes the point, though somewhat ungraciously, as follows: " I am quite ready to allow it (the coffer) to be 'a blind sarcophagus,' viz. : a *deceiving blind* to the eyes of the profane Egyptian workmen, as well as a symbol sarcophagus to others, reminding them of death, judgment, and eternity (as well taught by William Simpson, artist), but without therefore interfering one iota with its farther more exact objects and intentions." (*Our Inheritance in the Great Pyramid*, 1874, p. 142.)

There is, in this passage, an innocent unconsciousness on the part of the professor, of the inconsistency, not to say dishonesty, imputed to the designers of the mysterious pyramid coffer, which is truly amusing. Their "exact object and intention" was to make manifest to men the will of God as to the measures they should use in their daily intercourse with each other, by the construction of a type and standard of such measures to be copied and employed by them ; but their *act* was to place before men "a deceiving blind," adapted to remind them, not of bargaining and selling, but of " death, judgment, and eternity." This same imputation of inconsistency between purpose and act, ascribed to the builders, appears as well in the writings of John Taylor as in those of Prof. Smyth. Mr. Taylor has the following curious paragraph (we quote from "*Our Inheritance*," etc., p. 98, not having found the passage in place in Mr. Taylor's book): " The quarter corn measures of the British farmer are fourth parts or quarters of the contents of the coffer in the King's Chamber of the Great Pyramid ; and the same pyramid's name, instead of being descended from πῦρ, *fire*, may rather have been derived from πυρός, *wheat*, and μέτρον, *measure*, signifying a measure of wheat. To establish the groundwork of an international standard to that end, *though not at that time to publish it generally*, would seem to have been a leading purpose of the Great Pyramid ages ago; and the true value in size of its particular measure has not sensibly deteriorated during all the varied revolutions of society in the last 4,040 years." How far this last assertion is sustained by the facts will presently be examined.

Since, therefore, it is admitted that this vessel of which the character has been so laboriously discussed, and of which the metrological purpose is so hotly insisted on, has never had any other figure than that which it has now, the injuries by recent violence excepted, we should have a right to expect that, taken as a measure of capacity, it should be taken for what it will hold now, or rather what it would have held when originally shut up uninjured in its finished form in the heart of the Pyramid. But this is not the doctrine preached to us by the disciples of the Pyramid faith. The coffer, they say, as a standard of capacity, must have the parts which have been cut away in giving it the form of a sarcophagus, restored, so that all its sides shall be equal in height and in thickness. With this understanding it ceases to be an actual present standard, but becomes merely an ideal standard. It is not an instrumentality for ascertaining experimentally the quantity of matter which constitutes an unit of bulk; but it affords the means of calculating what that unit ought to be. The elements entering into that calculation have been furnished by means of measurements made by many explorers, and especially by Prof. Smyth himself, who has devoted to this inquiry an immense amount of painstaking labor. The several dimensions so ascertained, when expressed in English inches, seem to be connected with each other by no clear law of relation, nor are they improved in this respect when converted into what Prof. Smyth calls Pyramid inches; but John Taylor has found that, when expressed in *digits*, a digit being the twenty-fourth part of a royal cubit of 20.736 British inches, the interior length is, or was apparently meant to be, 90 digits, the breadth 30 digits, and the depth 40 digits.

The contents, as computed by Prof. Smyth according to different methods, which it is hardly worth while to repeat, vary from a little above to a little below 71,250 cubic Pyramid inches, which are equivalent to 71,464 cubic British inches. Now the cube of the double cubit of Karnak (41.472 inches) is 71,328.8 cubic inches; so that Mr. Taylor's inference that it was the design of the constructor of the coffer to give it the capacity of a double cubit cubed seems to have a foundation of probability. But this simple solution of a very simple problem is by no means satisfactory to Prof. Smyth. He discovers a much more recondite origin for this particular number. His method involves the use, it is true, of two uncertain quantities; and perhaps it may be regarded as evidence of a too fastidiously critical mind to remark that such elements are out of place in fixing a standard of absolute accuracy. These elements are, first, the polar axis of the earth, which, as we have seen, is still a subject of controversy, and secondly, the earth's mean density, which is more unsettled still. Prof. Smyth's proposition is this: Multiply the tenth part of the cube of the ten-millionth part of the earth's polar diameter by the mean density of the earth, and the product will give the Pyramid unit of capacity—that is to say, the contents of the coffer as it was before it was cut down into a sarcophagus. Now the ten-millionth part of the polar diameter of the earth is held, by the disciples of the Pyramid religion, as we have seen, to be a double sacred cubit, equal to 50 Pyramid inches, or 50.05 British inches. And by trial we shall find that $\frac{1}{10} \times 50^3 \times 5.7 = 71,250$ cubic Pyramid inches, and that $\frac{1}{10} \times 50.05^3 \times 5.7 = 71,464$ cubic British inches. The arithmetical coincidence is exact: but we shall see that this extremely satisfactory result is only owing to the happy selection of a value for the axis of the earth which no computer has ever found, and of a number expressive of the earth's density which no investigator of that subject has ever reached. The question of the earth's axis we have already considered. Let us attend for a moment to the other. The density of the earth is a very difficult subject of investigation. It has been sought by three methods: 1. By observing the effect of the lateral attraction of a mountain upon the direction of the plumb-line—a method employed by Maskelyne, and by Col. Sir Henry James; 2. By measuring the amount of torsion produced by bringing heavy leaden balls near the small balls of a delicate torsion-balance—the method of Cavendish, repeated by Reich and Baily; and 3, by comparing the relative numbers of diurnal oscillations of the same pendulum at the earth's surface and in deep mines—the method of Prof. Airy. The results obtained by the different experimenters have been widely different.

Maskelyne inferred a density of 4.71; James, a density of 5.316; Cavendish, 5.32; Baily, 5.66; Reich, 5.58; and Airy, 6.56. Supposing all these determinations to be of equal weight, the probabilities would favor their mean, which is 5.524. But they are not of equal weight; and though the name of Airy is a great one, the practical difficulties in the way of applying his method place his results among the least reliable. From a careful study of this question more than ten years ago, the present writer was led to the conclusion that the mean density of the earth cannot differ far from 5.6. Prof. Newcomb says: "Of these results that of Baily is probably the best, and the most probable mean density of the earth is about $5\frac{2}{3}$ times that of water." But if we use Baily's mean density 5.66, we shall obtain, by Prof. Smyth's process, only 70,750 cubic Pyramid inches for the contents of the coffer—a value which will never answer. And if, instead of 50.05 British inches as the ten-millionth part of the earth's polar axis, we take the mean of the last five computations of that axis, which we have already given, and employ the ten-millionth part of this, viz., 49.273 British inches, along with Baily's density, in Prof. Smyth's formula, the totally discouraging result is arrived at of 67,865 cubic British inches.

The *rationale* of Professor Smyth's process, of which it is almost sad to see here the disgraceful breakdown, seems to be the following: In the Pyramid metrology, the passage from the linear base (in this case, the sacred cubit) to the system of derivative measures, is not first, as is usual, to a measure of liquid capacity, but to an unit of solid capacity; neither is it to a solid, or vessel, having the usual form and magnitude of a cube of the linear base; but to a magnitude described as the tenth part of the cube of a double unit. This solid unit is supposed also to have a density equal to the mean density of the earth, so that if its volume is multiplied by the numerical index of the earth's specific gravity, the product will be the volume of a body of water having the same weight as the solid. And the volume of water thus obtained becomes in its turn the standard of the entire system.

It is impossible to believe, without evidence of the most positive and conclusive description, that a plan so complicated, so contrary to all metrological usage elsewhere, and, we may add, so singularly illogical, can ever have originated among any people; and yet here we are called upon to impute such a plan to a people who lived six thousand years ago, and of whom we have not a single fact, or a single line of record, to tell that they ever made a study of metrology at all.

The theory of the coffer by Professor Smyth seems to require no further attention. Let us now turn to the question how far Mr. Taylor's statement is capable of being maintained, viz., that the capacity of the coffer is the original unit of corn-measure, from which the measures still existing in Great Britain under the names of the *quarter* and the *bushel* have been derived; and that "the true value in size of its (the coffer's) particular measure has not sensibly deteriorated during all the varied revolutions of society in the last 4,040 years."

The British quarter, Mr. Taylor tells us, is the fourth part of an unit now obsolete, equivalent in capacity to the coffer, and which was called the *chaldron*. He even gives us the etymology of this name, deriving it from *caldarium*, the Roman warm bath; in allusion to the form of the coffer, which resembles a bathing-tub. How the Romans should have known the form of this vessel, which was shut up out of their sight until several hundred years after the fall of the Western Empire, or how they should have recognized it as a standard if they had seen it, since Professor Smyth tells us that it was intended as "a deceiving blind," not to be recognized, does not appear. Let that matter pass. What we have to inquire now is whether it is true that the present British corn-measures are measures originally derived from the coffer of the Pyramid; and how far it is true that, through such measures, the standard furnished by the coffer has been maintained without sensible variation for four thousand years.

We have no clear history of British weights and measures going back farther than about six hundred and fifty years (9 Henry III, A.D. 1225), though it is believed that the yard was determined in 1101 from the length of the arm of King Henry I. The earliest statute on the subject founded the whole system of British metrology upon the weight of the silver penny, which it required to be equal to that of "thirty-two wheat corns taken from the middle of the ear," the succession being that "twenty pennyweights do make an ounce; and twelve ounces one pound; and eight pounds do make a gallon of wine; and eight gallons of wine do make a London bushel, which is the eighth part of a quarter." If this quarter was the fourth part of the capacity of the Pyramid coffer, the king and his council seem not to have been aware of the fact. But was it? The thirty-two wheat corns were equal to 22½ grains Troy, and the bushel computed from these data had the capacity of 1691.52 cubic inches. From this we compute the quarter to have been equal to 13,532.16 cubic inches, and the chaldron, or assumed equivalent of the coffer, 54,128.64. Mr. John Quincy Adams, however (*Report to U. S. House of Rep.*, Feb. 22, 1820), says that in 1304 there was in actual use in England a wheat gallon of 264½ cubic inches, giving a bushel of 2,114⅔ cubic inches, from which we derive a quarter of 16,917⅓ cubic inches, and a chaldron of 67,669⅓ cubic inches.

In the reign of Henry VI, we find, A.D. 1423, a bushel of 2,148.24 cubic inches, afterward, with a very slight alteration, called the *Winchester bushel*. This gives a quarter of 17,185.92 cubic inches and a chaldron of 68,743.68 cubic inches.

Near the close of the same century (12 Henry VII, A.D. 1496) the bushel was reduced to such a degree that the people refused to use it. It was made 1,792 cubic inches, giving a quarter of 14,336 cubic inches, and a chaldron of 57,344 cubic inches.

During the same reign there came into use, somewhat irregularly, a bushel of 2,224 cubic inches, from which we may calculate a quarter of 17,792 cubic inches, and a chaldron of 71,168 cubic inches.

By a statute of Henry VIII (23 Henry VIII, A.D. 1531) a gallon was established of 282 cubic inches, giving a bushel of 2,256 cubic inches, a quarter of 18,048 cubic inches and a chaldron of 72,192 cubic inches.

In the year 1701 (13 William III) the Winchester bushel was reëstablished as the standard; but the bushel measure representing it found at the Exchequer proved to be too small, and the statute therefore explicitly defined the capacity of this measure, declaring that the standard bushel should be a cylindrical vessel 18½ inches in diameter and 8 inches deep. This statute was reënacted in the following reign (5 Anne, A.D. 1706), and the bushel, computed according to the terms of the act, contained about two cubic inches more than it had done originally, under the statute of Henry III. It was now 2150.42 cubic inches, from which we derive a quarter of 17,203.36 cubic inches, and a chaldron of 68,813.44 cubic inches.

Finally, in 1824 (4 George IV), it was enacted that the gallon measure shall be a vessel capable of containing "ten pounds avoirdupois, or 70,000 grains Troy, of distilled water at the temperature of 62° F., weighed by brass weights under the barometric pressure of thirty inches;" the volumetric capacity being at the same time stated at 277.274 cubic inches, from which it is seen that the bushel becomes 2218.192 cubic inches, the quarter 17,745.536 cubic inches, and the chaldron 70,982.144 cubic inches.

This brief outline of the history of British legislation on the subject of weights and measures will serve to show how completely independent it has been of the metrology of former centuries, and how entirely controlled by the immediate circumstances and needs of the British people. The earliest British corn-measure was based on the natural though imperfect standard of a definite number of wheat corns taken by weight. And the standard which for four centuries, ending in 1824, was generally prevalent in the British islands, and which continues still to be standard in the United States, gives a chaldron more than 2,500 cubic inches less than the capacity of the Pyramid coffer. In view of these facts, to say that this coffer has been the standard from which the corn-measures of Great Britain have been derived, and from which there has been no material variation for forty centuries, is one of so surprising a character as almost to argue lunacy in the man who makes it.

Of the Pyramid coffer as a standard of capacity measures, enough has perhaps been said; but there remains one observation to be made in regard to it too important to be omitted, the more especially as it seems not to have occurred hitherto to any writer on the subject on either side of the question. It is this: If this object was really intended to be a standard of capacity measures, it evinces, on the part of its designers, an astounding ignorance or a most culpable disregard of the principles which ought to govern such a construction. The use of a standard measure of any kind is implied in its name. It is to serve as a means of adjusting, by comparison, measures of similar character to be employed by the people in the daily transactions of business. An absolutely essential requisite of such a standard, therefore, is that it shall be of such moderate dimensions and inconsiderable weight as in the highest degree to facilitate manipulation. The same properties are equally necessary in order that it may easily lend itself to the processes necessary to test, from time to time, its own accuracy.

Among all enlightened nations, at the present time, capacity standards are tested by ascertaining experimentally the weight of distilled water they will hold when completely filled, the quantity being determined by weighing at a given temperature and under a given atmospheric pressure, with counterpoises also of given specific gravity—this last condition being required in order that allowance may be made for the weight of the air which these counterpoises displace. Moreover, in order to secure the accurate filling of the vessel, a peculiar artifice is resorted to. The unaided eye cannot be depended on to ascertain this point; for, on the one hand, in consequence of the property called capillarity, the fluid creeps up the walls of the vessel making it higher at the edges than over the general surface, so that the vessel may seem full before it is really so; and, on the other, in consequence of the property of viscosity, the vessel may be made heaping full without running over. In order to avoid either of these errors, the expedient is adopted of grinding the upper edge or rim of the vessel to a true plane surface and preparing for it a plate-glass cover, also ground to a true plane. Then, when the vessel is apparently full, the cover is placed over it. If it is heaping full the excess of liquid will be expelled, and the volume of water remaining will represent the exact capacity of the measure. But if the filling had not been complete, the deficiency will appear in the form of a bubble of greater or less magnitude, which, by artifices familiar to experts, may be brought to the middle of the glass cover, where there is a small orifice through which the confined air escapes, and through which, also, the deficiency of liquid may be supplied. This vessel, thus filled, after being carefully dried on the exterior, is placed in the balance and weighed. The difference between the weight thus found and the previously ascertained weight of the empty vessel and cover will be the weight of the contained water.

Now, in order that a process of this kind may be conveniently carried on, it is important, indeed indispensable, that the vessel shall be as light as is consistent with the preservation of its figure, and that it shall be easily portable as well when full as when empty; so that a standard-measure of capacity of such ponderosity as to be beyond the strength of a man to lift either full or empty, is nothing less than a preposterous absurdity. Tried by this test the pyramid coffer was either never designed to be a standard-measure, or it was the work of stupid dolts who had not the slightest idea of what a standard should be. The measurements of Prof. Smyth inform us that, in round numbers, this vessel measures externally, in length, seven feet six inches; in breadth, three feet three inches; and in height, three feet six inches. The same authority tells us that the interior capacity is equal to just one-half the entire solidity of the block whose external dimensions are above given; and as the specific gravity of Egyptian granite is 2.654, we are able to compute that its weight, when empty, is equal to 6,855 pounds avoirdupois, and, when full, to 9,434 pounds. That is to say, this prototype capacity-measure for all the world weighs nearly three and a half tons, and the volume of water required to fill it weighs one and a quarter tons—the whole weighing together four and three-quarters, that is to say nearly five, tons.

After this it is hardly worth while to remark on the folly of shutting up a measure intended for a standard in the heart of a mountain of rock, so as to be accessible only through a series of absolutely dark passages four hundred feet long, most of which a man can only traverse by crouching or crawling, and which were, moreover, so effectually plugged up by the builders less than one hundred feet from the entrance, that, but for the violence of a Mussulman caliph, the world would never even have known of their existence. Still less necessary is it to remark on the isolation of the object from all sources of water, or the absence of means of distillation, or of ascertaining weights, if water were present.

We may therefore very safely conclude that this object is by no means what Prof. Smyth calls it, "a deceiving blind," that is to say an apparent sarcophagus only, and a real measure of capacity. It is, on the contrary, plainly what it professes to be —an honest, outspoken, truth-telling sarcophagus, and nothing else.

The pretensions of the coffer as a measure of capacity having been thus so thoroughly disposed of, it is hardly necessary to say anything of it further as a standard of weight or of length. But there is something so defiant of common sense in the manner in which the theorists have looked at this side of the subject, that it can hardly be passed wholly in silence. The weight of water which the coffer will hold is the Pyramid ton, which is the theoretic Pyramidistic unit of weight. But inasmuch as, for practical purposes, a liquid measure of weight is an absurdity, the theorists find an equivalent solid by dividing the capacity of the coffer by 5.7, the assumed mean specific gravity of the earth. The result is a solid Pyramid ton of the bulk of 12,500 cubic inches of an imaginary material having a density equal to the earth's mean density. The principle of *fiveness* then seems to demand that five cubic inches of this substance, being the twenty-five hundredth part of a Pyramid ton, should stand for the practical unit in the petty transactions of everyday life, viz., the Pyramid pound, a weight undoubtedly convenient, since it exceeds the pound avoirdupois only by an amount a little less than half an ounce. But the material of which this type-weight is to be formed is so unfortunately chosen that there is no substance anywhere to be found upon the face of the earth, nor in its crust so far as it has been penetrated, which is fit for the purpose. That which comes nearest to the density required is metallic arsenic, of which the specific gravity varies from 5.62 to 5.96; but this substance, to say nothing of its noxious properties, is without tenacity or malleability, and is nearly as brittle as glass. Nor could such a material have been prepared artificially by a combination or alloy of metals, for the specific gravity of every metal known before the nineteenth century (*except arsenic*, as above mentioned) is higher than 7, and that of many much higher.

Thus in the metrological system of the Pyramid, the prototype standard of weight is a pure creation of the fancy, of which the practical realization is impossible.

Considered as a standard of length, the coffer is more illusive still. If it had been designed to furnish a standard of this sort, common sense would seem to dictate that, in some one of its dimensions, indeed, if not in all, it should directly illustrate the value of this standard. But neither in its length, its breadth, or its depth, whether measured externally or internally, do we find the sacred cubit, or a multiple or simple fraction of that measure; more than that, we do not even find, in any one of these dimensions, a round whole number of Pyramid inches. But the genius of the Pyramid theorists rises above these petty difficulties. The standard of length is in the coffer notwithstanding; and this is the way in which it is evolved to light. The capacity of the coffer having been divided as above, by 5.7, the earth's mean density, it is revealed to us that the resulting 12,500 solid cubic inches, the Pyramid ton, have exactly the volume of one-tenth of the cube of a double sacred cubit. We have only, therefore, to multiply the number just mentioned by ten, and then a simple extraction of the cube root will furnish us the standard of length required.

Even, however, after we have successfully accomplished this arithmetical operation, we are a good way off from the material and tangible working standard through which only any system of metrology can be practically useful to the human race.

In now regarding this metrological theory of the coffer as a whole, one cannot fail to note how completely it is penetrated through and through with the stamp of a modern invention. It is ingenious, no doubt, but its very ingenuity condemns it; for it betrays the immense amount of labor and study it must have cost to build up a consistent, and in so many respects plausible, system out of materials so insignificant and meagre; but just in proportion as, under the hands of the enthusiastic inventors, the system grows in elaborateness and symmetry, in the same proportion the probability fades away that the builders of the Pyramid ever entertained the least conception of such a creation.

But if it is really necessary to suppose that the constructors of this wretched stone box imagined that they were making anything more important than a receptacle for the mouldering remains of a mortal man, it seems to me that the numbers connected with it suggest what Prof. Smyth would probably call "a much grander reference in science" than any scheme could be, however ingenious, for regulating the petty traffic of the wine-shop and the butter-market. I make this appear as follows: Prof. Smyth has pointed out (*Our Inheritance*, etc., p. 188) that 5,151.65 Pyramid inches is the length of the side of a square equal in area to a meridian vertical triangular section of the Pyramid, or to a circle having the height of the Pyramid as a diameter. Now the capacity which he prefers to give to the coffer is 71,250 cubic Pyramid inches; and this number, stated as a decimal, is the logarithm, in our common system (omitting the index), of 5,158.3. which, regarded as British inches, are equivalent to 5,153.1 Pyramid inches. The coincidence is very close, and the slight discrepancy will be seen to be of no significance when we take into account the following considerations:

1. The capacity 71,250 has been adopted by Prof. Smyth, not because it is the exact result of any computation, but be-

cause it corresponds conveniently to his theory of the *fiveness* of the Pyramid. He has evidently no confidence in the exactness of the results obtained by immediate measurement; and his distrust is justified, since the surfaces measured are not plane but more or less concave, and the fiducial edges have for the most part disappeared. He therefore assumes a value for capacity which is "somewhere among" (a favorite method of his) those actually obtained, though it corresponds to no one of them, nor even to their mean. His different values are derived from a theory, which seems to be exalted to the dignity of an article of faith, that the interior capacity of the coffer is, and was intended to be, exactly one-half the volume of the original block, which we see still unaltered in its outside dimensions. The three values of the capacity hence obtained are as follows:

1. From direct interior measurements.................71.317 cu. in.
2. From direct exterior measurements (one-half)......71,160 "   "
3. From sum of bottom and sides directly measured.....71,266 "   "

How little reliance can be placed on these measurements may be judged from the fact that the mean of the first and third of the foregoing results, which, on any theory, ought to be equal to the second, is 71,291.5 cubic inches—that is to say, 131.5 cubic inches in excess. The mean of all the three values is 71,247.7 cubic inches, and this is so satisfactory to Prof. Smyth that he expresses himself in regard to it thus complacently: "Here then we have a vessel whose cubic contents are not only something excessively near to 71,250 cubic Pyramid inches, but it was pretty evidently intended to be both of that quantity within some minute fraction, and to carry a check and witness thereto down through all fair accidents, through all ages to distant time." (*Our Inheritance*, etc., p. 145.) If, therefore, 71,250 is not the exact logarithm of the side of the square above described, it is because, in the first place, it is not the exact value of the coffer's capacity.

2. The area of the meridian triangular section of the Pyramid depends materially upon the dimensions assumed for the base. Prof. Smyth has adopted 9,140 British inches, equal to 9,131 Pyramid inches, for his base measure; not because any investigator has ever found that measure, but because the number is necessary to his theory of the sacred cubit and the days of the tropical year. But, as the measurements given by

different authorities differ as widely as between the 9,110 British inches of Mr. Inglis, and the 9,168 of Col. Howard Vyse, I trust that, since Prof. Smyth has taken the liberty to adopt a dimension favorable to his theory, I may be allowed a similar liberty in regard to mine. If, then, the side of the base be assumed to be 9,142.8 Pyramid inches, as it suits me to assume it, the side of the square equal in area to the triangular meridian section will be 5,158.3 Pyramid inches, and in this case 71,250 will be its true logarithm.

3. But, inasmuch as we have seen that 71,250 cubic inches is not the capacity of the coffer, but only the capacity which Prof. Smyth guesses the coffer ought to have, and was probably meant to have; and as we have further seen that the real purpose of the constructor was, apparently, to make it of the capacity of a double royal cubit cubed, while the cube of the double cubit of Karnak a little exceeds the mean of Prof. Smyth's results; since, moreover, it has appeared that the royal cubit in actual use was sometimes a little longer and sometimes a little shorter, so that the double cubit used in the entrance passage seems, according to Prof. Smyth's measurements, to have varied from 41.46 to 41.63, while in the King's Chamber it was 41.25 or 41.26, we may be justified in assuming the double cubit employed by the constructors of the coffer to have been a trifle shorter than the Karnak rule, which latter, as we have seen, is 41.472. If we put it at 41.454, we shall obtain a theoretic capacity of 71,236 cubic British inches; which number taken decimally is the logarithm of 5,156.7 British inches, equivalent to 5,151.55 Pyramid inches, differing but a tenth of an inch from the side of the square in Prof. Smyth's calculation.

It is very clear to me, therefore, that, while the builders of the Pyramid designed to furnish, in the general external form of the structure, a visible and tangible solution of the knottiest problem of plane geometry, the quadrature of the circle, it was their purpose, in the construction of the coffer, to display their familiarity with the powerful algorithm of which we mistakenly ascribe the invention to the seventeenth century, and which we associate with the illustrious name of Napier, or in its ordinary form, with the less illustrious one of Briggs.

We have now passed in review all the really important points of the Pyramid faith. If these cannot be sustained, what remain are not worth the breath their discussion would cost. In fact, if the doctrine of the divine authority of the coffer alone breaks down, the whole theory tumbles together. We will nevertheless consider briefly the topics of secondary importance not yet disposed of.

The first of these is the latitude of the Pyramid. It is regarded by the theorists as a significant fact that this structure was, or was intended to be, placed upon the thirtieth parallel of north latitude. No evidence is presented of the probability of this purpose, in the minds of the builders, except that the monument happens to be pretty near to that parallel; and that parallel has certain relations to the geography and meteorology of the globe which have been discoveries of the later centuries, and which we are justified in pronouncing with great positiveness to have been, so far as they are true, wholly unknown to the human race until within a comparatively quite recent period. These are 1st, The thirtieth parallel divides into two exactly equal portions the surface of the hemisphere, land and water included, between the equator and the pole. 2nd, The thirtieth parallel enjoys a mean climatic temperature which is that of the entire habitable world. 3d, "Taking the distribution of land and sea in parallels of latitude, there is more land surface in the Great Pyramid's parallel of latitude than in any other." (*Our Inheritance*, etc., page 67.)

In regard to the first of these points it may be remarked that no evidence exists to show that the globular figure of the earth had been recognized by the Egyptians of the time of Khufu, or that, if it had been, that they had any acquaintance with the geometry of the sphere. If to this it should be replied that the emplacement of the monument was not intended to be significant to the men of that time, but to us, we may rejoin that we have no need of it, since all that it could tell us had been known to Western Europe some centuries before the sagacity of Prof. Smyth succeeded in detecting and making clear to us what were the secret purposes of the Egyptian mind six thousand years ago.

As to the second point, it is simply impossible that the slightest conception should have been entertained of such a science as comparative climatology in the age of pyramid construction, or that any differences of climate had ever been observed at all, except as they might affect personal comfort. That the pyramid builders should have placed their structure on the thirtieth parallel because that is the latitude of the earth's mean temperature is simply an impossibility, because, even if that were true, they knew nothing about temperatures, still less about mean temperature even of a particular locality, and a great deal less still about the mean temperature of the planet. The ancient Egyptians knew nothing of countries outside their own, except of those with which they were brought into contact by wars, and these were limited to Lybia, Ethiopia, Arabia and Syria, all of which were climatically much of the same character.

But it is not correct to say that the mean temperature of latitude $30°$ represents the mean temperature of the entire earth. If this should accidentally be true in one longitude it would probably not be so in any other; for parallels of latitude are nowhere isothermal lines: and the isotherm of $58°$ F., which, according to Prof. Dove, represents the mean temperature of the earth, is near latitude $40°$ in the Atlantic Ocean, and down as low as $30°$ on the coast of China; passing through Constantinople about eight hundred miles north of Cairo. Upon Guyot's meteorological maps, the isotherm passing through lower Egypt, near Cairo, is that of $72°$ F. Thus, if it was intended to mark by the Pyramid the region of the earth's mean temperature, its actual location was a blunder.

But, in point of fact, the Pyramid was not erected on the thirtieth parallel. It is actually more than a mile too far south. Two explanations have been given of this error: they should perhaps be called apologies for it. The first is that, as the latitude was probably determined by observation of Alpha Draconis (the pole star at that time), and as, in consequence of the refraction of the atmosphere, of which the builders knew nothing, the apparent altitude of the star was greater than the real altitude, the latitude observed was in excess of its real value, and hence the site was thrown too far south. To which we may reply, first, that the explanation is inadequate, since the correction for refraction, though it diminishes the error, fails to eliminate it; and secondly, that a divine illumination which had revealed to these men such difficult truths as the exact length of the earth's axis, and the correct distance of the earth from the sun, could hardly have failed them in so simple a matter as a question of terrestrial latitude.

The second of the apologies above referred to is equally unsatisfactory. It is that the pyramid was placed as far north as the extent of the Gizeh plateau would allow, and was even crowded up to the extreme northern brow of the declivity; but that this fell more than a mile short of the thirtieth parallel. This is a very lame explanation. If, as we are taught to believe, it was among the conditions prescribed by the Supreme Being, that the monument should be built on the thirtieth parallel of latitude, then either the Gizeh hill would have been under that parallel, or some other site would have been sought in which the condition might be fulfilled. The divine purpose could never have been baffled.

The probability, however, is that the builders never thought of the latitude at all. The pyramid, wherever built, must have been on or near some parallel. It might as well have been the parallel of thirty as any other. The Gizeh hill was chosen because it was a good place to build on. That is all the explanation of the emplacement needed.

The particular longitude of the pyramid's site seems to be regarded by the true believers as no less important than its latitude. If the structure were to be merely a metrological standard, one fails to see why it could not subserve its purpose as well in one country as in another. There seems, however, to have been an overruling necessity that it should be built in Egypt and nowhere else; and hence its builders were impelled ("led by the Spirit of God," Mr. Taylor says) to leave their own country in the plain of Shinar, and "to undertake the fulfillment of the great design" in that foreign and to them hostile land. For that it was hostile, both Mr. Taylor and Prof. Smyth concur in testifying, when they seek to identify its rulers with the Shepherd Kings of the middle dynasties, concerning whom history is so nearly silent, but who are mentioned in one of the fragments of Manetho, still extant, as follows: "We had formerly a king whose name was Timaos. In his time it came to pass, I know not how, that God was displeased with us; and there came up from the East, in a strange manner, men of an ignoble race, who had the confidence to invade our country, and easily subdued it by their power without a battle." These were the Shepherd Kings, who, having mastered the country, shut up the temples, and, as tradition asserted in the time of Herodotus, inflicted such cruelties upon the inhabitants that their memories were held in after ages in detestation, and people refused even to speak their names. Mr. Taylor, however, shrewdly suspected that these rulers were hated, not so much because they were bad, as because they were good—that is to say, pious—while the people who hated them were bad—that is to say, idolators, indignant at the closing of their temples. Along with them came certainly, as Mr. Taylor believes, the thirteen sons of Joktan, of whom the youngest was Jobab or Job, whom the same writer endeavors to identify with the afflicted man of Uz. After describing at some length the character of this people, Mr. Taylor goes on to say regarding them: "There could have been no motive sufficient to allure such a people as this to the banks of the Nile, according to the views usually taken of men's conduct. To build sepulchres of so vast a size in which no human being was ever laid—to build them for their own sepulchres, and then to leave them as soon as they were completed, in order to go to some other country for the rest of their lives, and there to be buried in obscure graves—is too absurd a supposition to be entertained concerning any rational creatures; and that these men were wise above most others is shown by their works. To build storehouses for corn of so vast a bulk, without leaving in them any chambers capable of holding corn, or accessible to persons bringing it, even if the chambers were large enough, is to attribute to the founders of the pyramids a degree of folly of which no people in the world were ever capable. For one purpose alone does it seem reasonable to conclude that any men should have undertaken so prodigious a labor, without looking for the slightest advantage to themselves; and it is that purpose for which we have seen so much evidence adduced as to force us to conclude that it must have been the end for which the pyramids were formed, viz., that they might serve as a record and memorial to the end of time, of the measure of the earth; and secondly, form a standard of measures of length, capacity and weight to which all nations might appeal as to a common authority, in their dealings with each other. But to attribute to the founders so grand and liberal a design, is to affirm that they were the greatest philosophers and the greatest benefactors the world ever knew."

It would be difficult to find, throughout the whole range of English literature, a proposition more ludicrously absurd than that which is embodied in the last sentence of the foregoing paragraph. The grandeur and liberality of the design manifested in the creation of the pyramid, consisted in the lavish prodigality with which human labor and the wealth wrung from the hard hands of a suffering people, were squandered in heaping up a monstrous pile of stone, from which its builders "looked for not the slightest advantage to themselves," and which, it may be added, could not possibly be of the slightest advantage to anybody else. Instead of being styled "the greatest philosophers," they would rather deserve to be stamped, unless some better interpretation of their work shall be discovered than has yet appeared, as the greatest dunces of antiquity. And when pæans are raised to them as "benefactors" of mankind, we may reasonably inquire whom they have benefited. Not certainly the generation whose miserable lives were crushed out of them in the intolerable toil exacted for the erection of these stupid structures. Not those who successively lived and died during the thousands of years in which the mysterious chambers of these monuments remained sealed against all intrusion from the living world. Not Al Mamoun, who with infinite labor penetrated into these same mysterious chambers, to find there, as his only reward, a huge and meaningless stone box, with or without a lid. Not ourselves, among whom these titanic structures have served no better purpose than to provoke unprofitable speculations and to stimulate brains which might be better employed, in weaving fantastic theories with which to clothe very ordinary objects with mystery. Not anybody has been benefited by them, from the beginning down to this day; nor, it may be added, could anybody have been benefited by them, if every dogma of the Pyramid religion had been literally true.

For it would be difficult to persuade a sane man that there is anything more intrinsically salutary to mankind in one particular measure or length, or of weight, or of capacity, than in any other. The properties which make any metrological system beneficial, are not the particular values of its units, but the relations of its denominations, uniformity in its practical applications, and facility of verification of its standards. The Pyramid system has never been in use and never will be; so there is nothing to be said upon either of the first two points. And as to the facility of verification in this system, it will probably be admitted, after what has been said above in regard to the coffer, that the possibility does not exist.

To return to the Shepherd Kings; as it is perfectly established by modern researches that the intruders so called belonged to the fifteenth, sixteenth and seventeenth dynasties, while the Pyramids were built by the rulers of the fourth, Prof. Smyth finds himself constrained to give them up. But he says: " That these *later* or 15th., 16th., and 17th., dynasty Shepherds did not build the Jeezeh, or indeed any of the Egyptian, Pyramids, does not by itself overthrow the whole theory or possibility of there having been an *earlier*, or quite distinct, Shepherd invasion, or temporary rule of Hyksos in lower Egypt, and perhaps even during the fourth or chief Pyramid building dynasty; for pastoral tribes existed in the East from the earliest times, and were much endued with tendencies to western emigration." (*Our Inheritance*, etc., p. 421.) While it surprises us a little to find Prof. Smyth here attributing the migration of the Pyramid builders to an unintelligent instinct, or native tendency, while Mr. Taylor tells us that they were "led by the spirit of God," we know, nevertheless so well what are the "tendencies" of the Professor, that, after this outgiving, we feel quite confident he will presently find what he wants. We are not disappointed; he quotes a little further on (p. 430), the following from Herodotus, which, in his view, clears up the whole difficulty: " They (the Egyptians) commonly call the Pyramids after Philition or Philitis, a shepherd who at that time fed his flocks about the place. This shepherd Philition becomes presently Prince Philitis; and then, after reciting the words in which Manetho, speaking of the Hyksos of the middle dynasties, makes them return to the East and build there a great city, our author proceeds to say, with what strikes us as a singularly cool perversion of history, *we have here as much as testifies to the earlier and truer Shepherd Prince Philitis* (the italics are ours), after having long controlled King Shofo during the very time that the Great Pyramid was building—to that Prince Philitis, I say, the leaving the country with a high hand, or by special agreement, with all his people and flocks—proceeding to Judea, and building there a city which he called Jerusalem." The name Jerusalem awakens a new association in the impressible mind of our Professor. He is reminded of " Melchizedek, further called king of Salem, which some consider to have been Jerusalem." He does not, in so many words, assert that Prince Philitis *was* Melchizedek; but he says that " he must have been, as to age, standing, country, and even title, very much such an one as that grandly mysterious character." And though he remarks that "the Bible does not indeed directly mention Melchizedek's ever having been sent into Egypt on any special mission (the Bible in fact names Melchizedek historically only in one single passage)—the grandest of missions, if there to erect or procure the erection of a prophetical monument which was only to be understood in the latter days of the world; but was destined to prove the inspiration origin, and Messiamic character of its design to both religious and irreligious," yet we can see that he entertains no doubt either that Prince Philitis was in effect the builder of the Pyramid, or that Melchizedek was Prince Philitis (*Our Inheritance*, etc., p. 433).

These Biblical discussions have led us a long way off from the question of the Pyramid's longitude with which we began. But the importance of this question of longitude must have been, in the minds of the Pyramid builders singularly great, since if we are to believe the disciples of the faith in our own day, it was sufficient to induce them to undertake a migration of nearly a thousand miles, to attempt and accomplish the conquest of all Lower Egypt, to hold the country for a long period of years, and then to abandon it and go to establish themselves finally in a third country which they must have wrested in like manner, as they had wrested Egypt, by violence, from its lawful possessors. The only palliation which can be suggested for these successive acts of robbery, is to be found in the consideration that the army of Prince Philitis or of King Melchizedek, being engaged in the fulfilment of a divine mission, had a right of appropriation over such lands as they fancied, which was superior to the natural and merely human right of property.

To return to the question of longitude, from which these Biblical discussions have carried us away farther than we intended; what is there, we may inquire, in the longitude of Gizeh, which should make it indispensably necessary that the Pyramid should be erected under that meridian, and no other? What is there about that meridian to call for the sacrifice of home and country on the part of a nation, or at least a very numerous tribe, for a migration in mass, and a painful march of a thousand miles, for armies, conquest, the subjugation of a peaceful country and the enslavement of its unoffending inhabitants, and for the expatriation of the conquerors for more than a century, in the accomplishment of a mission connected with it? Certainly there must have been some object to be attained, of incalculable importance, to justify this subversion of the foundations of society, this great movement of the nations, with all the wide-spread suffering which must have inevitably attended it. There was such an object, as our friends of the Pyramid persuasion inform us—an object of transcendent importance—an object which, when they reveal it to us, makes us hold our breath in admiration, and lay our mouths in the dust in silent conviction—it was in order that "the most magnificent, disinterested and glorious work that was ever conceived and executed by mankind" might be erected under a meridian of which it may be said that "there is more earth and less sea in that meridian than in any other meridian all the world round." To an argument so overwhelming in its force as this, of course, not a word can be uttered in reply.

It is a pity, nevertheless, that the proposition here stated is true only in the limited sense in which, by the word *meridian*, we understand a geographical semi-circle extending from pole to pole. If, however, we are permitted to define this word to mean an entire great circle of the sphere passing through the poles, there are several meridians which pass over more of *terra firma* than that of Gizeh. This is true, for example, of the meridian 60° W.—120° E. of Greenwich; also of the meridian 80° W.—100° E.; and of the meridian of New York City, which is nearly that of 75° W.—105° E., which last apparently possesses in very truth the property claimed for that of Gizeh, of having under it "more earth and less sea than any meridian all the world round." It is, therefore, to be regretted that Melchizedek, who probably knew nothing of meridians, nor anything even of geography beyond the region lying between and including Chaldæa and the valley of the Nile, had not been inspired to continue his westward march until he had found the meridian which enjoys really the distinction which belongs to that of Gizeh only in a qualified sense; since in that case the discovery of America might have antedated Columbus by three or four thousand years, and we might have had the Great Pyramid in our own Central Park.

The next point of the Pyramid faith which we have to examine is that which relates to this monument as a standard of temperature. In natural caves, and in artificial excavations beneath the surface of the earth, the extremes of heat and cold become less divergent as we descend; and at a quite moderate depth become merged in one common temperature, the temperature due to the locality, which remains invariable throughout the year. That such a constant temperature should prevail in the heart of so large a mass of masonry as the Great Pyramid, is not improbable; that it would do so in the chamber left unfinished by the builders deep down in the rock beneath the base, is almost certain. But that that fact or probability was known to the builders, or that it was among the considerations which induced the erection of the structure, is a great deal more than doubtful. It is as nearly certain as anything not absolutely demonstrated can be, that they knew nothing whatever about heat and cold beyond the fact that the extremes of either are painful to the sense. The art or science of thermometry originated in the seventeenth century. None of the nations of antiquity, however enlightened, neither the star-gazing Chaldæans, nor the cultured Greeks, nor even the world-subduing Romans, though they pushed their conquests equally among the snows of Dacia and northern Gaul, and over the burning sands of Lybia and Ethiopia, had any notion of it. It is hardly probable that the Egyptians of the thirty-seventh century before our era were more advanced than these. But if they were, where is the evidence of it? How is it that, among all the relics of Egyptian art, and Egyptian science, and Egyptian life, that have been gathered together at Boulak, there is no fragment or trace of a thermometric instrument; or that among all the thousands of papyri and mural inscriptions that have been deciphered since our century began, not one makes mention of temperatures or their measurement? And if the builders really intended that the temperature of the King's Chamber should be accepted by posterity as a representative and exemplification of what they believed to be the mean temperature of the planet, why did they not in some form or other say so? Why, moreover, if they intended this standard temperature to be a term of comparison, did they devise no means by which comparisons could be made? What possible advantage could it be to any one to know that the temperature of the interior of this mountain of rock is so and so, unless he can be able to say that the temperature of some other place is higher or lower? He must either carry the place into the pyramid, which is impossible, or contrive some means of carrying the temperature of the pyramid to the place, or that of the place to the pyramid.

No evidence, or trace of evidence, of the existence of such instrumentalities is to be found. Prof. Smyth, indeed, talks coolly and confidently enough about "the two hundred and fifty degrees of the Great Pyramid scale" (*Our Inheritance*, etc., p. 260), meaning 250° between the freezing and boiling points of water; quietly assuming that there was such a scale; for no other reason that appears, except that the interior temperature is, as he assumes, that of 68° F., which is one-fifth part of the distance on the scale from 32° F. freezing, to 212° F. boiling; and that to divide this total interval into 250 parts would be more convenient than the division of either Fahrenheit, Reaumur, or Celsius, besides affording a beautiful illustration of his theory of the *fiveness* of the Pyramid. Now if the Pyramid builders had really a thermometric scale of this sort, it is truly a mystery defying explanation, that they neglected to contrive some effectual method of transmitting a knowledge of it to posterity, since they could not have reasonably anticipated that there would arise, after the lapse of some six thousand years, a genius sufficiently gifted to read, with the single clew offered by the constant temperature of the King's Chamber, their entire thermometric system, and to vindicate for them the glory of its authorship.

Only, unfortunately, Prof. Dove, the highest modern authority in meteorology, says that the mean temperature of the earth is 58° F. instead of 68° F., and the mean annual temperature of the Nile Delta is 72° F., and not 68° F.; neither of which statements is in harmony with the Pyramidistic property of *fiveness*.

It remains only to consider for a moment the astronomical significancy of the Pyramid. Very grave importance has been attached to this, chiefly because of the light it is presumed to throw upon the date of the erection. Two facts are relied on to demonstrate the relations of this monument to astronomy. They are (1) its true orientation; and (2) the inclination of its passages. As to the first of these facts, it is indisputable. The bounding lines of the Pyramid are directed more truly to the cardinal points of the compass than those of any other known structure erected by man before the invention of telescopic sights. The meridian established by Tycho Brahe, at his famous observatory of Uranienborg, has been found by more recent examination to have had an azimuthal error exceeding fourteen minutes, while the error of Pyramid orientation was determined by Prof. Smyth's repeated and careful observation to be less than five minutes (4′ 35″), or not one-third so great. This near approach to exactness, however, would not necessarily imply large astronomical knowledge, or a high degree of astronomical science, on the part of the builders. The idea of laying down a true north and south line by observation of the extreme eastern and western elongations of any conspicuous star near the pole, might easily occur to even an ignorant man, although considerable skill would be required to carry out the idea in practice.

The question, however, will naturally arise, why should the builders desire to give to their work this true orientation? Not certainly in order that the pyramid might be used as an observatory; for, in its completed condition it offered but one outlook toward the heavens, and that only in a direction less than four degrees from the pole; while for any practically useful purpose in astronomy, after the question of orientation had been settled, there could be no more utterly unprofitable species of observation than that of a close circumpolar star. If there was really a purpose in this apparently very careful adjustment of the faces of the pyramid toward the cardinal points, it would be difficult to conjecture its motive, unless we adopt the very plausible suggestion of Mr. Proctor, that the Pyramid was an astrological monument, and that its peculiarities were determined by the horoscope of the monarch who caused it to be constructed.

An astronomical significancy has been ascribed to the inclined entrance passage of the Pyramid, for no better reason than that it looks out toward a point of the heavens not very far distant from the pole of diurnal rotation. It has been already remarked that no conceivable purpose of interest to astronomical science could be subserved by observation in this direction after the position of the meridian line had been fixed; and it is certain that no advantage of any kind was derived from it after the completion of the Pyramid; since its mouth was closely sealed, and remained for centuries undiscovered. If, therefore, the inclination of this passage was really determined by any serious motive, and was not a result of mere hazard or caprice, we seem to be driven to conclude that it was designed to answer only some temporary end which ceased to have an interest after the work was done. We can conceive of no such end, unless it were the adjustment of the orientation of the building. This, in the opinion of Mr. Proctor, is the true explanation both of the north and south and direction of the inclination of the entrance. He supposes that an approximate north and south line was first found by raising a somewhat lofty and pointed upright upon a level plane ; and then, at the moment of meridian passage of a circumpolar star, setting up another shorter one behind it, so that the tops of the two might exactly range with the star. The line connecting the uprights would then be a north and south line, subject to such inaccuracy as might naturally result from uncertainty, in the absence of artificial timekeepers, of the true moment of meridian transit. A more correct determination could probably be made by observations of the star at the limits of its largest excursions to the east and the west, and dividing the angle between the two directions thus obtained. Mr. Proctor, however, thinks that "The builders would require a much more satisfactory north and south line than this," and he asks, "What, at this stage of the proceedings could be more perfect, as a method of obtaining the true bearing of the pole, than to dig a tubular hole into the solid rock, along which tube the pole star at its lower culmination should be visible? Perfect stability," he adds, " would thus be ensured for this fundamental direction-line. It would be easy to obtain the direction with great accuracy even though at first starting the borings were not quite correctly made."—(*The Great Pyramid*, by Prof. R. A. Proctor, New York, 1883, pp. 93, 94.)

All this is true, and it furnishes a plausible explanation of the facts. We can only say of it that a modern engineer would have found means to lay down a line above ground, just as stable, just as accurate, and at vastly less cost of time or labor or money. For it is to be observed that the boring of the tunnel, difficult as that work must necessarily be, is but a first step towards finding the meridian line by this method. The work could not but be difficult, since the cross-section of the tube in the case of the Great Pyramid was but 3 1-2 by 4 feet, while the length was more than 230, and the material was solid limestone, to be actually picked out by tools in the hands of men, unaided by any of the explosives which perform for the modern engineer the heaviest part of his underground work. But after the bore is complete, it is necessary in this process, in order to transfer the north and south line to the surface of the earth, where it is wanted, to make a second and vertical perforation at a point judged or computed to be just over the southern termination of the inclined tube, and through this to drop a plumb line, the suspending point of which is to be moved east or west as may be necessary to bring the plummet to the inclined meridian line in the tunnel below.

Now it is easy enough to see that if it had been only desired to fix by stable monuments a meridian line deduced from observation of a circumpolar star, it would have been cheaper and more expeditious to raise a column of masonry a hundred feet high, than to bore out of solid rock a tunnel two hundred and thirty feet long; so that the mode adopted by the Pyramid builders to fix their orientation was not creditable either to their science or to their good sense. Since, however, it is possible, I do not consider it by any means demonstrated, that the tube beneath the Great Pyramid was bored for the purpose asserted, it would seem as if it had fully answered its end before the building began, and that there was no need to continue it through the courses of the rising structure. Mr. Proctor, however, supposes that the observations for orientation continued to be repeated for every additional course; and hence he derives a reason of being for the ascending passage which rises at a similar angle toward the south. For if, just below the junction of the two passages, the descending passage had been stopped up, and the basin thus formed had been partially filled with water, the image of the star at its culmination might have been seen reflected from the surface of the water by an observer in the rising passage; and thus, after the structure, in the progress of building, had been raised above the northern entrance mouth, the observations for orientation might still have been carried on in the manner here suggested, by reflection. Of course, this is possible, but it would hardly seem to have been necessary.

The most important deduction from this theory of the design of the inclined passages, is that it implies the presence of a close circumpolar star in position to be observed through the entrance passage at the time of the erection of the monument. If there was such a star it could not have been our present pole-star, for that has only been brought, by the effect of the slow movement known as the precession of the equinoxes, into position to be entitled to its present distinction within the last few centuries. At a period so comparatively recent as the beginning of our era, it was still distant from the pole more than twenty-five degrees. By looking on a celestial sphere along the small circle of latitude which is distant about twenty-three and a half degrees from the pole of the ecliptic, we may easily find all the stars which have been near the pole during an entire precessional revolution of twenty-five thousand years, and select any which are conspicuous enough to have been regarded at any time as pole-stars. This has been done by the devotees of the Pyramid faith, and the star called Alpha Draconis has been fixed on as the pole-star of the Pyramid.

It becomes, then, a question of the first magnitude in point of importance to ascertain at what time this star may have been seen, by an observer placed far within, to pass the axis of the passage. Prof. Smyth computes the distance which, in order to do this, it should have had from the pole, by comparing the inclination of the passage with the altitude of the pole at the place. The inclination, directly measured, is made by him to be 26° 27′; but, as the ascending passage and the grand gallery have inclinations slightly different, the former being 26° 6′ and the latter 26° 17′ 37″, while it is presumed that the intention was to make them originally equal, he has chosen to take the mean of the three, viz., 26° 17′; and this, subtracted from 29° 59′, the elevation of the pole, gives 3° 42′ for the required polar distance of the star.

The star Alpha Draconis appears to have been first pointed out by Sir John Herschel as the probable pole-star of the Pyramid builders; but the manner in which he attacked the problem was by inquiring, not at what date the star was at a given distance from the pole, but how far the star was actually from the pole four thousand years ago, the computation having been made in 1839. Four thousand years counted backward from this date carries us to the year 2161 B.C. The calculation is given in detail in the Appendix to Col. Howard Vyse's great work on the Pyramids, Vol. II., pp. 108, 109, the resulting polar distance being stated at 2° 51′ 15″. There seems to be some error (perhaps of transcription) here, since, according to our computation, the star had this distance from the pole in 2359 B.C., or about two hundred years earlier than Sir John Herschel makes it. It is true, however, that the star had the polar distance of 3° 42′ in 2175 B.C. (Prof. Smyth makes it 2170 B.C.), so that, in that year, it might have been observed in the axis of the tube at its lower culmination. This, in the opinion of the professor, fixes the date of the foundation of the Pyramid. But there was a much earlier date at which the star was at this same distance from the pole, being then further west in longitude than the pole, as it had, in the other case, been further east. This was in 3503 B.C., a date only about two hundred years later than that assigned by Brugsch to Cheops, and therefore the more probable of the two, if this very doubtful astronomical theory of the Pyramid is to be accepted.

There seems, however, to be no good reason why the inclinations of the interior passages should be taken into account in this calculation. Since the builders have not themselves given us a reason for anything that they did, it is quite possible that the differences found in the inclinations of the several passages were intentional; and such extravagant claims have been made for these operatives in regard to the accuracy of their workmanship, as to make the supposition quite untenable that they could have committed positive errors so large as these differences imply. There remains the hypothesis that the angles originally given to the slopes may have been disturbed by movements of the earth within the past four thousand years. But this seems to be negatived by the observations made in 1865 by Mr. Inglis and Prof. Smyth on the floor-levels of the corner-sockets, which, to their astonishment, appeared to be quite true. Of the north-east corner socket Prof. Smyth remarks: "Mr. Inglis examined it over the whole floor with a spirit level. 'Why, I cannot find any error in it,' said he." (*Life and Work, etc.*, Vol. III., p. 529.) And of the south-east socket he observes (*Ib.*, p. 538): "Besides the astonishing firmness of the foundation, the truth of level was such that on removing from the north-east to the south-east socket there was hardly more than half a turn of any one of the fine-threaded foot-screws to be made to put the instrument level within a second of space." There have been, therefore, no earth movements in Lower Egypt for the past four thousand years. We should, accordingly, take 26° 27′ as the true original inclination of the entrance passage, and should hence seek a date for a polar distance of the star of 3° 32′. But this is of no great practical importance, since it makes a difference of date of only about thirty years.

The probability, however, appears to be that the inclination of the passages had nothing whatever to do with astronomy, and that all the labor that has been expended over the star Alpha Draconis has been thrown away. This probability rests

(1) upon the well known fact that an inclined entrance passage on the north face is a feature common to all the pyramids, which must have an explanation (if it could be found) applicable alike to all. Col. Howard Vyse has given the angles of inclination of the entrances of each of the nine Pyramids of Gizeh, as follows:

NAME.	ANGLE.	NAME.	ANGLE.
Great Pyramid,	26° 41'	Fifth Pyramid,	27° 12'
Second "	25° 55'	Sixth "	30° 00'
Third "	26° 02'	Seventh "	33° 35'
Fourth "	27° 00'	Eighth "	34° 05'
		Ninth "	28° 00'

To these may be added:

NAME.	ANGLE.
Pyramid of Abou Roash	22° 35'
Great Pyramid of Saccarah	23° 20'
Third " " "	26° 35'
North Stone Pyramid of Dashour	27° 56'
South " " "	26° 10'
North Pyramid of Abouseir	27° 5'
Great " " "	26° 3'

Now if it had been the purpose of the inclined passage of the second pyramid of Gizeh to observe the star Alpha Draconis in its axis, at the lower culmination, since the star would have then been 4° 04' from the pole, the Pyramid must have been built either in 2111 B.C., that is to say, sixty years later than the Great Pyramid, or in 3567 B.C., that is to say sixty years earlier than the highest and most probable of the dates astronomically indicated for the former. But if anything is settled in Egyptian archæology, it is that these two pyramids were built by two brothers.

Should it be thought that the interval of sixty years is not enough to discredit the belief that these two monuments might be the work of brothers, let us take the Fourth Pyramid, and it may be shown by the same mode of reasoning that this must have been erected as early as 2403 B.C., that is to say more than two hundred years before the Great Pyramid. And in like manner the North Stone Pyramid of Dashour dates back to 2515 B.C., or to about three hundred and fifty years earlier than the Great Pyramid. The Southern Stone Pyramid at the same place would appear to have been erected almost contemporaneously with the Great Pyramid of Gizeh; and this monument has also the interesting feature of a western as well as a northern entrance, with an angular descent of 26° 36'. Had such a passage been found in the Great Pyramid, we should probably have been instructed that it was intended for observations in the Prime Vertical; though it might have been found difficult to account for its particular angle of inclination.

The entrance passage of the Sixth Pyramid of Gizeh is directed to a point within one minute of the pole. Inasmuch as the star Alpha Draconis, at its closest appulse, is distant from the pole nearly nine minutes, it follows that it can never have been seen in the axis of this passage; although, about the year 2840 B.C., and for a long time before and after, it must have been within the field of view to an observer in that passage throughout the entire twenty-four hours.

There is therefore no good reason for believing that these passages were constructed for astronomical purposes, and their general similarity forces us to believe that their actual purpose, whether we can explain it or not, was everywhere the same. It cannot have been for the orientation of the Pyramids, for though this is generally nearly true, it is not true without exception; the Great Pyramid of Saccarah, according to Col. Vyse, deviating as much as 4° 35' from the true north and south, and the Third Gizeh Pyramid being out nearly a quarter of a degree.

It is to be presumed, however, that the particular inclinations given to the several passages, were determined, as is usual in building to a batter, by the proportion arbitrarily adopted by the builders between base and altitude. In the same way, no doubt, was determined the side slope given to the faces of the Pyramids themselves. Thus the masonry core of the Great Pyramid of Gizeh was apparently built to a batter of four base, to five perpendicular; and the same rule was apparently followed with several of the remaining pyramids of the Gizeh group.

The entrance passages of the first four Gizeh Pyramids were probably built to a batter of two base, to one perpendicular. The exact observance of this rule would give 26° 34', which is precisely the mean between the measurements of this inclination given by Col. Howard Vyse, as above, *viz.*, 26° 41', and of Prof. Smyth, *viz.*, 26° 27'. In the practical work of construction, however, measurements would have to be made with severer accuracy than can reasonably be hoped for with stone masons, in order to secure in the results exact conformity with the trigonometrical indications.

In the Sixth Pyramid the rule may have been eight base, to five perpendicular; and in the Seventh and Eighth five base, to three perpendicular.

The hypothesis above stated in regard to the Great Pyramid is supported by the testimony of Prof. Smyth himself. The subjoined, Fig. 2, is a copy of Fig. 2, Plate VII., given in

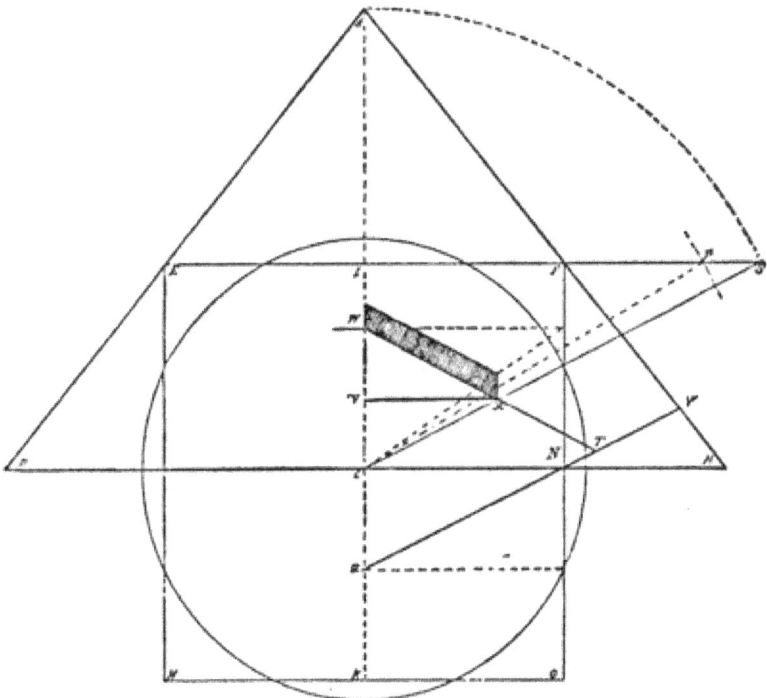

LENGTH AND PLACES OF PASSAGES IN THE GREAT PYRAMID.

Trisect *IG* & Bisect *CR* by horizontal lines, then *ZY* parallel to *CS* marks entrance passage. *WT* at an equal but opposite angle marks First Ascending passage and the Grand Gallery. Angle *BCP* (where *CP* = side of equal area square) = 30° = Latitude, approximately.

the work so often quoted in this paper, *viz.*, "Our Inheritance," etc., and designed to illustrate certain geometrical re'ations which do not concern us here. In this figure *ABD* is a vertical meridian section of the Great Pyramid. *EFGH* is a square equal in area to the triangular section, placed with its centre at *C* in the middle of the base, and its sides, *EF* and *GH*, parallel to the same. *CK*, equal to the half side of the square, is bisected in *Z*, making *CZ* equal to one-quarter the side of the square. Then CS is drawn to make the angle BCS equal to the inclination of the entrance passage, *viz.*, 26° 17′, and ZY is drawn parallel to CS. ZY is then coincident in direction and in position with the entrance passage, and it cuts the base at the point N, where the side FG of the square also cuts it. Now CN is twice CZ; that is to say the inclination of the entrance is determined by the mechanical process of building to a batter of two base to one perpendicular. This illustration, moreover, accounts not only for the angle of inclination of the entrance, but for its exact position in the building; and thus demonstrates that its construction was determined, in every particular, by purely geometrical considerations, and without any regard to astronomy at all.

There is but one point in the construction of the Great Pyramid which, in the mind of a man in possession of his sober senses, can justly be regarded as connecting it in any manner with exact science. It is the fact that it appears to possess, or very nearly to possess, that property which has induced Prof. Smyth to give it the name of a π Pyramid—a pyramid, that is to say, in which the perimeter of the base is just equal to the circumference of a circle having the height of the pyramid for a radius. It cannot be said that this point has been fully made out. It has been inferred from measurements of the angular slope of the side of the Pyramid. This angle, if the proposition is true, ought to be equal to 51° 51′ 14.3″. In the present denuded condition of the monument, it is impossible to test the question by direct observation upon the visible faces; but the angles on the casing stones, fortunately found in place by Col. Vyse in 1837, gave by one method of measurement 51° 50′, and by another 51° 52′ 15.5″. The mean of these is 51° 51′ 7¾″, which very nearly approaches the exact angle required. Prof. Smyth has endeavored to corroborate this result by many angular observations, made upon both the sides and corners of the monument in its existing state, estimating for the thickness of the casing removed—a very uncertain method—with results which, to him at least, are entirely satisfactory. It is perfectly obvious, nevertheless, that practical builders could never build to an angle like this—the impossibility strikes us the more forcibly when we see how difficult it is by direct measurement of the stones found still in their original condition, to ascertain to what angle they really did build. Practical stone masons need for their guidance a rule requiring the use of only their ordinary measures of length. If they had built to the batter of four base, to five perpendicular, the result would have been a slope of 50° 21' nearly. If they had used the rule of twenty-five base, to thirty-two perpendicular, the slope would have been 52°.

The builders seem to have been guided by a rule resembling one of these—probably by the first, corrected and checked by a more exact rule applied at the corners. For it has been noticed that the angle of the corners is exactly that corresponding to a base of ten and a perpendicular of nine, from which is deduced a lateral slope of 51° 50' 39", differing from the required π inclination by only 35.3". Now it has been very plausibly suggested by Col. Sir Henry James, that the building process was probably conducted by first setting out the courses at the angles in accordance with the rule of ten base, to nine perpendicular, and then carrying the courses along the sides by line and level. The resulting height of the Pyramid constructed by this process, as compared with that of a true π Pyramid of the same base, is given by Prof. Smyth in Pyramid inches, as follows: "Using the same base side length (9131 Pyramid inches) for both—by the 10 : 9 hypothesis, 5811 by the π hypothesis, 5813," showing a difference of only two Pyramid inches—that is to say, a quantity quite imperceptible in so enormous a mass. There can therefore be no doubt that the process by which the Pyramid was actually erected was that which is here described, and that, if the Pyramid is, as it very probably is, a π Pyramid, it is so by accident.

In conclusion, it is impossible not once more to revert to the singular fact that, if all the wonderful things are true of the Pyramid that have been asserted of it, not one scintilla of evidence has been produced to show that any one of them was ever in the mind or the intention of the builders at all. If they had intended, as Mr. Taylor says they did, to make this structure "a record and a memorial to the end of time of the Measure of the Earth;" if they had intended to convey to posterity, by means of it, a knowledge of the exact length of the earth's axis, of the exact number of days in the tropical year, of the exact error of the British inch, of the exact number of inches in the sacred cubit, of the exact distance of the earth from the sun, of the earth's exact mean temperature, of its exact specific gravity, and of the exact ratio of the radius of the circle to its circumference, it exceeds all the bounds of reasonable credulity to suppose that they would fail to leave—not to say a clear, distinct, and unmistakable enunciation of such a purpose—but the slightest trace, character, emblem or token of any kind, to bear witness to their intention.

But the case is far stronger than this. Not only have they furnished us voluntarily no evidence of a design on their part to convey a message to posterity, not only have they failed to give us a hint of their possession of any important knowledge which they might convey if they would, but they have endeavored to prevent, by means the most effectual which they knew how to employ, any discovery by future generations of the secrets, whether important or trivial, which they had locked up in the heart of this mountainous mass of stone. Not only was the external opening of the single entrance passage so carefully closed up that it remained undiscovered for an unknown number of centuries, but the passage branching from this and leading to the chamber containing the only object of interest in the whole structure, was plugged up at its lower extremity with blocks of solid granite measuring in section about three and a half feet by four, and fifteen feet in total length; which were made tapering so as to fit closely, like a massive wedge, into a passage similarly tapering, and into which they were let down from above, and strongly cemented as well as driven. The point of the entrance passage at which this ramification took place was also carefully concealed, by closing the opening with a triangular block of stone like that which forms the facing of the passages, and made to appear on the interior to be a continuation of the facing. Nothing can be more palpably evident than that it was the determined purpose of the constructors of this monument not only not to inclose in its secret chambers any messages of any kind whatever to future generations, but to render it practically impossible that anything shut up in those chambers should ever be known to mankind to the end of time. Their measures were judiciously taken. It was no fault of theirs that they proved ineffectual at last.

I have met with some persons who, while they have felt sensibly the absurdity of the pretensions set up on behalf of the Pyramid, have nevertheless appeared to be considerably shaken by the numerous coincidences which its theory seems to present with certain well ascertained truths, such as for instance, the near approach to a decimal relation between the British inch and the axis of the earth, the approach to a similar relation between the height of the Pyramid and the distance of the sun, the position of the star Alpha Draconis four thousand years ago, the approximate equality of the obsolete British chaldron, and the computed capacity of the coffer; these, and other things like them, constitute a combination of analogies which such persons can hardly bring themselves to regard as wholly accidental. But from what has been said above, it has been made, I trust, to appear that the coincidences here assumed to exist are in some cases really non-existent; that in other cases they are far from being so close as asserted, and that in other cases still (as in the π property of the Pyramid) they are capable of very simple explanation, and are strictly accidental in the sense that the result was not intended or anticipated by the producer.

But in order to show how easily a system like that which I have called the theory of the Divine Legation of the Pyramid, may be built up out of the most unpromising material, I will make a supposition. Ephesus, a city of Asia Minor, consecrated to Diana, was one of the most splendid of the Grecian cities of antiquity. Its principal temple, erected to its patron goddess, was of so surpassing magnificence as to have been assigned a place among the seven wonders of the world. This splendid edifice, originally founded in the last year of the fifty-sixth Olympiad, after having stood for nearly two hundred years, was willfully fired by a miscreant named Herostratus, who avowed under torture, that the only motive for his crime was the hope to immortalize his own memory. After the battle of Ipsus, in the third year of the 119th Olympiad, Lysimachus, one of the allied victorious commanders, got possession of Ephesus, and commenced a reconstruction of the city nearer the site of the temple, which had been erected without the walls at a distance of seven stadia. The rebuilding of the temple was a part of this scheme of reconstruction, and this was early commenced, but was not brought to completion for more than two centuries. In A. D. 262, this new temple was once more destroyed by the Goths, and its ruins became a quarry of material for modern buildings, out of which cities so far off even as Constantinople drew supplies. So complete, with the lapse of time, was the disappearance of this once majestic architectural pile, that there remained at length not a trace of its existence above ground, and the very site where it had stood became matter of doubtful conjecture.

It is now fifteen or twenty years since Mr. J. T. Wood, an architect in the service of the British government, entered upon a series of explorations of the points in and about Ephesus which seemed to promise to throw light upon its ancient history. He succeeded in uncovering the foundations, beneath more than seven feet of earth, of the latest temple, and under this those of two others, the earliest at a depth of twenty feet, but all of equal dimensions. He also unearthed the foundations of a great theater, and those of an Odeon, or Music Hall, all of unknown antiquity. Of these several edifices he took measures as well as he could, and these measures are what interest us at present.

He found the temple to be 343 British feet long, and 164 feet wide; the theater to be 495 feet in diameter, and the Odeon 153 feet. I propose to treat these measurements as Prof. Smyth has treated those of the Pyramid. And, in the first place, in order to make the parallel complete, I must suppose that other visitors have followed Mr. Wood, and have made independent measurements of the same constructions. We should naturally look for differences in any case; but in this case the situation of the object must have made the measurement unusually difficult and doubtful. I would not intimate that all the difference between Pliny, who reports the dimensions of the temple as 425 and 220, and who wrote in the first century, A. D., and Mr. Wood, whose results are given above, is due to the inaccuracy of the British architect entirely, for I presume the Roman wrote from hearsay; but it is a fact of common observation that different tourists who visit many other objects besides the Pyramids, give us often very discordant reports of the dimensions of such as they profess to have measured with their own hands. Prof. Smyth has found that even men usually so exact as the French academicians, Messrs. Jomard and Denon, were capable of committing a grave error—an error amounting to several inches—in so simple a measurement as that of the height of the coffer in the King's Chamber.

I suppose, then, that the length of the Ephesian temple has been measured by four different visitors besides Mr. Wood, and that their results are 342.6 ft., 343.7 ft., 344.3 ft., and 344.9 ft. These with Mr. Wood's 343 ft. give a mean of 343.7 ft., as the most probable length. Reduced to inches this gives us 4,124.4.

Now, considering that this temple was consecrated to Diana, who is, in other words, Luna, or the moon, and having been taught by Prof. Smyth, how the dimensions of the Pyramid are mixed up with the days of the year and the axis of the earth, I feel satisfied that we must have something of the same kind here ; only that, instead of the days of the year we ought to have the days of the lunation, and instead of the axis of the earth we ought to have the axis of the moon. The lunation is about 29½ days long, and accordingly I divide 4,124.4 by 29, and I find the quotient to be a little over 14. Fourteen inches, therefore, I conjecture to be, probably contained " a round decimal number " of times in the moon's diameter. I proceed to test this probability.

It is to be considered that when this temple was built the magnitude of the moon could have been but imperfectly known. Though the nearest to us of all the heavenly bodies, the determination of its dimensions must, in the infancy of astronomy, have presented peculiar difficulties. It is a problem involving three independent elements, no one of them easily ascertainable—the moon's mean apparent angular diameter, her mean equatorial horizontal parallax, and the earth's equatorial diameter. Many of the estimates or computations of this quantity twenty-five hundred years ago (since the Ephesians, being heathens, could have had no supernatural light to guide them) must have gone wide of the mark. We know this value now with all desirable accuracy. It is very close to 2160 English miles. But, in the fifty-sixth Olympiad, estimates must have varied through a range as wide as from 2000 to 2400 miles, or even wider. We may assume, therefore, 2205 miles as a probable mean between these estimates. This, reduced, gives 11,642,400 feet, or 139,708,800 inches.

I see, then, that the ten-millionth part of the moon's diameter is equal to 13.97 British inches, and I call this ten-millionth part a *lunar ell*.

I will now suppose that some one of the explorers whom I have imagined to have followed Mr. Wood, has found in a cavity of some hollow masonry, the interior of which has been exposed to view in the progress of decay, a measuring rule uniformly divided, and evidently one of those used by the builders, but which had been accidentally left there and forgotten.

I will suppose the divisions to be twenty-eight in number, and the total length to fall short of twenty-eight English inches by about six one-hundredth parts of an inch—in short, that it measures 27.94 inches. It is distinctly divided in the middle into two equal parts; and each part is further subdivided into fourteen equal divisions. I call these divisions lunar inches. The rule is evidently a double lunar ell; and the lunar ell contains fourteen lunar inches, each of which is equal to $\frac{466}{467}$ of an English inch; or is short of the English inch by the 467th, or nearly the 500th part.

If it should be objected that there is no such measure as a lunar ell in the metrological system known to have been in common use among the Greeks, the reply naturally presents itself that this measure was not in common use—that it was a sacred measure employed only in constructions connected with the worship of the Moon, and perhaps even in that use confined to the sacred city of Ephesus.

I have a suspicion that the length of the temple must contain a number of lunar ells which is probably a multiple of the number of days in the lunar month. In order to test this hypothesis I propose to find the number of lunar ells in 343.7 feet English. But remembering that the British inch exceeds the lunar inch by about one five-hundredth part, I first increase 343.7 by 0.6874 ft., the quotient of a division by 500, which gives a total of 344.3874. This number of feet becomes lunar ells by subtracting one-seventh part; inasmuch as a foot is six-sevenths of a lunar ell. One-seventh part of 344.3874 is 49.1972; and, the subtraction being made, there remain 295.1902 lunar ells. Now the lunar month contains 29.5306 days, so that the length of the temple appears to contain ten times as many lunar ells as there are days in the lunar month.

In order to make the comparison a little more exact, let us calculate how many English inches there are in as many lunar ells as the lunar month contains days. In English inches 13.97 is the value of a lunar ell. And 13.97 × 29.5306 = 412.5425. Also 343.7 English feet contain 4124.4 English inches; the tenth part of which is 412.44, identical with the former result to the tenth of an inch. It is therefore very clearly established that the intention of the builders of this temple was to make its length ten times the ten-millionth part of the Moon's diameter multiplied into the number of days of the lunar month. Or, to paraphrase the manner of speaking of Prof. Smyth, it is "equivalent to the architect having laid out the length of the temple with a measuring rod fourteen inches long in his hand, and in his head the number of days and parts of a day in a lunation multiplied by ten, coupled with the intention to represent that number of days in terms of that rod" in the largest dimension of the temple.

The division of the lunar ell into fourteen parts has a natural explanation. The Asiatic Greeks, like all other eastern peoples, were worshippers of the heavenly host; and though the Ephesians paid their chief devotion to Diana, they were not unmindful of the divinities associated with the other wandering stars. Of this class there were known to them only seven, viz.: The Sun, the Moon, Mercury, Venus, Mars, Jupiter and Saturn. Of these, two were the greater, and the remaining five the lesser lights. The number *seven* was, therefore, a number held in special reverence; and this number multiplied by two, the number of the greater lights, gave fourteen, the number of lunar inches into which the lunar ell was divided.

The numbers *two*, *five* and *seven* appear all to have been held in reverence by the Ephesians, the first as representing the greater lights of the heavens, the second as significant of the lesser lights, and the third as standing for the whole solar system so far as it was known to them. Their multiples naturally shared this distinction, as is illustrated in the lunar ell, and in the fact stated by Mr. Wood that the entrance to the temple is made by fourteen steps. Thus also is explained the partiality shown for round decimal numbers.

The breadth of the temple, determined in the same manner as the length, by taking a mean of several presumed measurements, may be put at 161.53 English feet, which would be equivalent to 161.85 lunar feet; the diameter of the Odeon at 151.862 English or 152.185 Ephesian, and the diameter of the theatre at 493.73 English or 494.72 Ephesian.

It seems to have been the intention of the builders to make the breadth of the temple ten times the lunar ell multiplied by the sacred number fourteen. The number of inches in 161.85 lunar feet is 1942.20. If we take the breadth at 163.3 (which would be "among" the measurements) we should obtain a result of 1959.6. But $14 \times 14 \times 10 = 1960$.

There is, however, a curious relation between the temple and the Odeon, involving also the length of the sidereal year. It is that the area of the temple floor is equal to the area of a rectangle of which one side is the diameter of the Odeon, and the other the number of sidereal days, integral and fractional, in the year, with an error of only about three ten-thousandth parts of a day. Thus 344.3874 × 161.85 = 55,739.10069 square feet, which number divided by 152.185 gives as a quotient 366.2588; the true length of the sidereal year being 366.2591.

The diameter of the Odeon seems also to connect the twenty-four hours of the day with the true length of the tropical year, for it appears that 152.185 multiplied by 24 gives, as a product, 365.244—a value in excess of the true value by two one-thousandths of a day.

The diameter of the theatre appears to have been designed to denote the date of the erection of the building. In a city consecrated to Diana it was natural that time should be reckoned by the lunar year. Such was the practice among all the early Greeks, those in Europe as well as those in Asia, as it was among the Egyptians, Jews, and Asiatics generally. The theatre was therefore founded sometime during the 495th lunar year counting from the common epoch, *i. e.*, from the beginning of the first Olympiad, 776 B. C. In order to find the corresponding solar year we must first ascertain the length of this year expressed in lunar months, by dividing 365.2422 by 29.5306, which gives us 12.368 as the number of lunar months in the tropical year. We state then the proportion, as 12.368 is to 12, so is 494.72 to a fourth term, which we find to be exactly 480. We conclude, therefore, that the theatre was founded in the 480th year from the epoch, which places the foundation in the last year of the 120th Olympiad, or in the fifth year after the reconstruction of the city was undertaken by Lysimachus.

This measure seems also to have been intended to embody the length of the mean lunation, for, on reducing it to inches and dividing by 29.5306, the number of days in the lunar month, we obtain a quotient of 201.00; that is to say almost exactly 200, or a number compounded of the round decimal multiple 100, and the sacred number 2. Probably, if we had an entirely correct measurement, the coincidence would be complete.

Furthermore, if we multiply the days of the tropical year by the sacred number 14, we shall obtain a product of 5113.3902. And if we suppose the theatre to have had a propylon in front, as it must have had, of say 16.62 feet in breadth, the entire measure, propylon included, multiplied by 10, will be the same, *viz.*, 5113.4.

These coincidences are sufficient to show that the Ephesians had very early become extremely proficient in astronomy, and that they had a fancy very much like that of the ancient Egyptians, which led them to build their astronomy (and we may add their piety) into their monuments. I regret that I have not a larger number of measurements for study and comparison. I cannot doubt that the results would be equally interesting. Unfortunately, I have not at hand Mr. Wood's full account of his discoveries. The foregoing particulars are derived from an article contributed by him to one of our cyclopædias.

But the most curious fact brought to light by this inquiry is that the lunar ell, taken as many times as there are days integral and fractional in the lunar month, gives a result which, reduced to English inches, is exactly 412.5425; while the length of the King's Chamber in the Great Pyramid, as determined by the mean of the very careful measurements of Prof. Smyth, made on both sides, is 412.54. This measure, which in its relations to the Pyramid is very important, I propose to call a lunar metron. As the breadth of the King's Chamber is half a metron, the whole perimeter is equal to three metra, representing one season of three lunar months. Reduced to Pyramid inches the metron becomes 412.13, a quarter part of which, *viz.*, 103.033, being the half breadth of the King's Chamber, figures in Prof. Smyth's calculations in so many ways that it is called by him "the unit test of the King's Chamber."

This unit test is contained twice in the breadth of the King's Chamber, four times in its length, and five times in its solid diagonal. It is exactly the length of the granite portion of the floor of the antechamber, and the height of the granite wainscot on the east side of the same. Multiplied by one hundred, it is the diameter of a circle whose area is just equal to that of the square base of the Pyramid. One half of this, *viz.*, 5151.65, is the side of a square equal to a vertical triangular section of the Pyramid, and also to a circle having a diameter equal to the Pyramid's height. And as the hundredth part of the Pyramid's height doubled is equal to 116.26 Pyramid inches, which is the entire length of the antechamber floor, while 103.033 is the length of the granite part of it only, it follows that the floor represents at the same time the side of a square and the diameter of a circle of equal area. "Or, as the Abbe Moigno" (we quote from *Our Inheritance*, etc., p. 187, in *Les Mondes*) "more elegantly puts it (having previously called $116.26 = 2r$, and $103.033 = c$): this remarkable employment of granite and limestone by the ancient Pyramid architect is the method adopted by him of saying, in the common language of mathematical science, from an isolated mountain peak of 4,000 years ago, to all nations in the present educated age of the world, that

$$\pi r^2 = c^2."$$

This is undoubtedly eloquence, but unfortunately the announcement comes at a time when it can be of no possible use, the fact stated having been well known to the world for several centuries. "Who," says the Abbé, "after this first coincidence of the antechamber, could pretend that the diversity of the materials and their relations, or *differences*, of length, are a simple brute accident?" Well, nobody, perhaps; but whoever imagines they are *not*, must, I think, be constrained to believe that the cunning contrivers of these ingenious scientific puzzles were not disciples of Melchizedek at all, but mere miserable heathen worshippers of Isis. For Isis was the Egyptian personification of the Moon; and the builders of the Pyramid were evidently acquainted with the lunar inch, the lunar ell, and the lunar *metron;* for they employed these measures not only in the King's Chamber, but throughout the entire structure.

Still one can suppose that the differences of length in the floor of the antechamber were not "a simple brute accident," without going so far to account for them as the worthy Abbé and his friend, Prof. Smyth, are supposed to do. It is a fact that the diameter of a circle and the side of its equivalent square are proportioned to each other very nearly as nine to eight. Eight-ninths of the length of the floor of the antechamber were laid down in granite, and the remaining one-ninth in limestone. Eight-ninths of 116.26 inches (the total length) is 103.342, which differs from the length of the granite portion as derived from measurement, only three-tenths of an inch. The constructors were probably not thinking of squares or circles at all.

One-tenth of the metron is the exact breadth of the entrance passage and of the first ascending passage. Two-tenths is the breadth of the grand gallery; one-tenth is the distance between the ramps of the gallery, and one-twentieth is the breadth of each ramp. The length of the Queen's Chamber is half a metron, and the height of its walls appears to have been intended to be in the mean the same, though the roof is gabled, and the measurements vary between 182 at the side walls, and 244 at the vertex of the gable. Finally, the side of the base of the Pyramid itself was probably laid out of a length of 220 metra; since 220×412.54 gives a result nearly approaching the base measurement of Mr. Inglis.

It appears, therefore, to be pretty clearly demonstrated that, if any religious considerations entered into the construction of the Pyramid, they were connected with the worship of Isis. And this hypothesis derives a high degree of plausibility from the historical fact that the Egyptians were a remarkably religious people.

I venture therefore to propose a new theory of the Pyramid, which may, with propriety, be styled a lunar theory. It is supported by evidence quite as striking as that which is adduced in favor of the theory of the divine legation, and of precisely the same kind. It is, as the other is not, entirely in harmony with what we know of the character of the ancient Egyptians, and it dispenses with the violent hypothesis of the invasion and subjugation of their country, and the cruel oppression of its inhabitants by a migratory multitude coming from the distant plains of Shinar, to fulfill a pious mission with arms in their hands. I do not anticipate the early or general acceptance of my theory. I content myself with the conviction that it is worthy to be accepted—or at least *as* worthy of acceptance as any which has been heretofore promulgated. And if I shall, though failing of such signal success, accomplish only so much as to induce some of my fellow men to apply a little common sense to the study of a subject which has been heretofore involved in an elaborate web of ingeniously contrived mysticism, I shall feel that my labor has not been wholly thrown away.

Postscript.

Since the foregoing paper was presented to the American Metrological Society, I have met with a recent work on the Pyramids and Temples of Gizeh, Mr. W. M. Flinders Petrie.

Had I made acquaintance with this book earlier, I should have spared myself the trouble I have taken; for, by the array of new facts which it presents, it demolishes completely the pretensions of the Pyramid religion, and buries, beyond all hope of resurrection, the ingenious theories of Mr. John Taylor and Prof. Piazzi Smyth.

But this is not what Mr. Petrie went to Egypt to do. When he visited Gizeh, his object was to carry out some lines of research which had been indicated by Prof. Smyth as still desirable in order to the more full confirmation of the theory set forth in his works. In his earlier life the author had been himself a true believer, and as the son of Mr. William Petrie, whose valuable contributions to the Pyramid theory are so frequently referred to, and so warmly commended by Prof. Smyth, he was necessarily trained from infancy in the orthodox faith. He manifested, in fact, so long ago as 1874, the sincerity and depth of his earlier convictions, by publishing a collection of "Researches on the Great Pyramid," evincing much study and labor, and prefaced in these words:

"The following researches on this monument confirm those distinctive principles of its design and construction first announced by the sagacity of John Taylor and Professor Piazzi Smyth, as they were set forth in Prof. Smyth's first publication on the subject, 'Our Inheritance in the Great Pyramid,' first edition, published just ten years ago. The many fresh facts here noticed, while showing much further and interesting development of those principles, add irrefragable proof of their validity as against superficial theories, old and new."

It will be admitted that very thick scales must have fallen from the eyes of the man who wrote that before he could see clearly to pen the following closing paragraph of his new work:

"As to the results of the whole investigation perhaps many theorists will agree with an American who was a warm believer in Pyramid theories when he came to Gizeh. I had the pleasure of his company for a couple of days, and at our last meal together he said to me, in a saddened tone, 'Well, sir, I feel as if I had been to a funeral. By all means let the old theories have a decent burial, though we should take care that, in our haste, none of the wounded ones are buried alive.'"

Mr. Petrie took up his residence at Gizeh in December, 1880, and between that time and April, 1882, devoted nine months of continuous work in making careful measurements of all the monuments of the group, and conducting a trigonometrical survey of the entire plateau. It would be impracticable to give here in detail the results reached by him affecting Pyramid theories; neither is it necessary, for no one who has been particularly interested in the subject will fail to read this book. I will content myself with citing two only of these results: the two which affect most vitally the inspiration theory of the Pyramid, viz., the dimensions of the Pyramid's base, and the cubic capacity of the coffer.

The length of the Pyramid's base side was determined by Mr. Petrie as Prof. Smyth might have determined it, and ought to have determined it, trigonometrically. He found the four sides equal, with a maximum difference from the mean of all the measurements of only about an inch. The north and south sides, between which the apparent difference is only a tenth of an inch, seem to be slightly in excess of the east and west; but the form of the base is sensibly a square. The side of this square has been hitherto the unknown quantity in the Pyramid religion, but it has been a fundamental article in the creed that it should measure just 9,140 British inches. By the inexorable laws of trigonometrical science it is proved to measure, in fact, only 9,068.8 British inches. With this determination, the beautiful union of the sacred cubit and the length of the tropical year melts away into thin air, to be heard of no more among men.

As to the coffer, its capacity is 71,960 cubic British inches; whereas, in order that it may be equal to the tenth part of a double sacred cubit cubed and multiplied by 5.7, it ought to be equal only to 71,464 cubic British inches, or to 71,250 cubic Pyramid inches. The error is only 500 cubic inches, but it is quite enough to secure for the standard unit of the Pyramid metrological system an early place far away in the limbo of forgotten things.

The cube root of 71,960 is 41.594, which exceeds the Karnak double cubit of 41,472 by 0.122, or hardly an eighth of an inch. This approach to coincidence is sufficiently near to make it probable that the constructors, if they were aiming at any determinate capacity, had in view the cube of a double royal cubit. Working in so difficult a material and in so early an age of human history, it should rather surprise us that their error was so small, than that it is so large.

The true measure of the base, while it does away with the fanciful notion of sacred cubits and days of the year, seems to suggest another possibility which, though it may be esteemed quite as fanciful, must nevertheless, if true, be regarded as no less honorable than that to early Egyptian science. The base of the hyperbolic system of logarithms (usually represented by the character e) is 2.71828. Let this number denote Pyramid inches, and it may be called an Egyptian palm. Then ten Egyptian palms will be 27.1828 Pyramid inches, approaching nearly to the Russian measure of length called an archine (pronounced *arsheen*) of 28 English inches exactly : and which may therefore be called a Pyramid archine. We are now to suppose certain numbers, from their relations to certain geometrical solids, to have been regarded as type numbers. Thus, if we take 1,000 as the type of the cube, $523\frac{1}{3}$ becomes that of the corresponding sphere, 500 that of the triangular prism or wedge, and $333\frac{1}{3}$ that of the Pyramid.

The north side of the great Pyramid has been found by Mr. Petrie to measure 9,069.5 English inches. Let us take this to the nearest even inch, 9,070, and reduce it to Pyramid inches by subtracting, according to Prof. Smyth's rule, the one thousandth part; the result will be 9,060.93 Pyramid inches.

Now my hypothesis is that the dimensions of the Pyramid's base were determined by making the side equal to the Pyramid archine taken as many times as there are units in the Pyramid type number. Thus, $27.1828 \times 333\frac{1}{3} = 9,060.93$, which is precisely the number of Pyramid inches found in this dimension as actually measured.

Had a discovery of this kind been made in the treatment of the orthodox, but unhappily fallacious, measurements of this monument on which the Pyramid religion has been founded, no doubt it would have been announced with great exultation, as a convincing evidence of the high degree of advancement in mathematical science which had been attained by the builders of the Pyramid, or of the preternatural light by which their hands had been guided.

I have already pointed out in the foregoing paper, the evidence furnished by the computed capacity of the coffer, of the knowledge possessed by these same architects of our common system of logarithms. This evidence disappears with the more exact measurement and computation of Mr. Petrie; but in its place arises the much more startling proof just given of their familiarity with the more interesting logarithmic system which, after their time, must have been lost to the world for some thousands of years, and was only re-discovered so late as the seventeenth century of the Christian era, by the ingenuity of Baron Napier.

This coincidence is so suggestive, that I am almost tempted by it to make a study of all the remaining measures of the Pyramid which Mr. Petrie has now at last given us correctly. Time fails me, however, and I must content myself with making a present of this discovery of mine to the apostles of the ancient Pyramid faith, with the expression at the same time of the hope, that they may find in it the fruitful germ of a new body of doctrine, to take the place of that which Mr. Petrie has so remorselessly swept away.

INDEX.

The exact place on the page referred to is indicated in ninths by the superior figure; *e. g.*, 18^3 means page 18, three-ninths from top to bottom.

(?) is prefixed to references to fanciful theories proposed by the author. (? ?) is prefixed to similar theories held by disciples of the Pyramid Faith.

The Temple, Theatre and Odeon referred to are those in Ephesus.

Abbreviations—K. C., for King's Chamber.
                M. S., for Metric System.
                P., for Pyramid.
                P:, for Great Pyramid.

Absurdity of Mr. Taylor's assumed object of P: 65^2–66^8; of the argument that the P: unit is a function of the earth's daily motion, 35^5–36^9.

Absurd System of metrology now in existence, 4^2.

Actium, date of battle of, recorded in P: (?), 44^9.

Adam, date of creation of, 38^1.

Adams, John Quincy, quotation from report to Congress of, on value in cu. in. of the wheat gallon, 54^3.

Adoption of metre as a basic unit of metrological system. 2^9–3^1.

Advent foreshadowed in P: (? ?), 43^1.

Airy's, Prof., method of finding earth's density, 51^9; determination of earth's density, 52^1; New method for determining solar distance, 32^{8-9}; mean determination of value of polar axis of earth, 26^7.

Aiton and Inglis, object of visit of, to Gizeh, 20^9; Measurements at Gizeh, by, 21^{1-3}; measurements of base of P: by, 19^4.

Alexandria, meridian of, 23^9.

Alexandrian Code, date of deluge by, 37^7.

Al Mamoun, results of association of with P:, 47^9–49^4.

Alpha Draconis, pole star of P: 14^2–16^8, 75^2. Position of 4,000 years ago, 15^3.

Alpha Lyra, 15^3.

Alphonsine Tables, date of annunciation by, 40^7.

Anne, Winchester bushel under, 54^6.

Antechamber, implicit quadrature of circle in floor of (?), 89^9–90^1.

Archæologists, different dates for deluge by, 37^4–38^2, for the dispersion, 38^{7-9}; for the annunciation, 39^9–40^9.

Archæology, evidence of the identity of the builders of P: and second P. of Gizeh in Egyptian, 77^{6-9}; coincidence of linear measures of P: and dates of sacred and profane history, 43^1–44^9; of P:, 37^9–46^9.

Archine, signification of, 94^2.

Arithmetical ingenuity of P: disciples, 16^9.

Asa, Terah defeated by, 46^4.

Asanides, king of Babylon, 46^1.

Auger, date of annunciation by, 40^9.

Astronomical significance of the Temple of Diana proposed (?), 89^{1-3}; of the P: (??), 71^7–78^9; of ascending passage and grand gallery of P: (??), 15^9–16^9.

Babel, date of dispersion of mankind at, marked by P: passages (??), 37¹, 37⁴, 37⁵⁻⁶.
Baily's method of finding density of earth, 51⁸; results, 52¹.
Barnard, earth's density determined by, 52³; "Metric System" by, 2⁴; date of erection of P: by, 75⁵.
Baronius' date of the annunciation, 40⁸.
Base of P: measured (??), 7¹; why not made by Smyth, 20⁴-23¹. See P.
Batter, proportions of, for seven pyramids of Gizeh, 78⁸-79¹.
        proportions of, for P:, 78⁸-80⁸.
Benefit of P: not yet exposed, 66²⁻⁴.
Bengel's date of annunciation, 40⁸.
Bessel's value of polar axis, 26⁸.
Bill to make metric system compulsory in Eng., 3³⁻⁷.
Brennus, prediction in P: of capture of Rome by (?), 46¹.
Brugsch, date assigned to Cheops by, 76³; date of Exodus by, 38⁹-39¹, 39⁷.
  "   History of Egypt under the Pharaohs by, 39⁸.

Cairo, built by outer covering of P:, 21⁸.
California, admission of to union predicted by the "ruled lines" (?), 46⁴.
Calvisius' date of annunciation, 40⁸.
Capacity, coffer in K. C. a measure of (??), 11⁴-12⁴; of coffer assumed by Smyth, 59⁹-60⁸; failure of Smyth's formula for unit of, 52⁴; methods for testing standards of, 56¹-56⁷.
Cavendish, method of finding earth's density, employed by, 51⁸; results, 52¹.
Chaldron, of less capacity than coffer of K.C., 55⁴; etymology of, and relation to coffer, 53⁴.
Chamber, *King's*, "unit test of," 89⁸.
Christ, date of birth of, marked by P: passages (??), 37³, 39⁸-40⁸.
Chronology of annunciation, 39⁸-40⁸; examples of curious coincidences of (?), 45⁹-46⁸; of Exodus of Israelites, 38⁸-39⁸; of P: expository of other systems of dates (?), 43¹-43⁵; of P:, theory of supported by dimensions of longitudinal passages (??), 36⁸-46⁸; of P: by Smyth, Bunsen, and Brugsch, 30³; of Theatre, how determined (?), 88⁶⁻⁷.
Circle, quadrature of, shown by the external form of P: (?), 61⁸.
Civilization, effect of on barter and trade, 1⁴.
Clarke, Col. A. R., published results of determination of polar axis of earth by, 26²⁻⁹.
Climatology, Comparative, not known to Egyptians, 62⁸-63⁴.
Clinton's date of the Exodus, 39⁷.
Code, Alexandrian, date of deluge by, 37⁷.
Coffer, 46⁸-61⁹; absence of lid of, 47⁷, 48⁸; capacity of according to Petrie, 93⁵⁻⁶; Smyth's estimate of capacity of (??), 59⁹-60⁸; Smyth's method of computation of (??), 50⁹-53¹; of greater capacity than the chaldron, 55⁴; difficulties of as a standard of capacity, 55⁸-57⁷; a measure of capacity (??), 11⁸-12⁴; ideality of, as measure of capacity, 50²⁻⁴; capacity of, given by Mr. Taylor, 51¹; capacity of, stated decimally (?), 56⁷-61⁸; different values of capacity of, 60⁴; design of builders of, 48⁸-49⁹; description of, 11¹-12⁴; dimensions of in P: digits, 50⁷⁻⁸; divine meaning of (??), 47¹⁻²; vital nature of doctrine of to P: theology, 62¹; measurements of, by Smyth, 57¹⁻³; secretion of, as a measure (??), 57⁴⁻⁶; *a priori* metrological purpose of P: (??), 50³⁻⁶; mutilation of, 48⁴-49⁸; nature of, 46⁸-47⁴; not a sarcophagus (??), 47⁴-49⁹; a blind sarcophagus (??), 49⁶⁻⁸; as expository of common system of logarithms, Mr. W. M. F.

INDEX.
99

Petrie's measurements bearing upon, 94^8-95^1; as a standard of length (??), 58^7-59^9; not a multiple of the sacred cubit, 58^{7-9}; author's theory of object of (?), 59^7-61^8; metrological theory of (??), 59^{8-9}; Taylor's theory of (??), 53^{3-6}; alleged relations of number and volume in (??), 12^4; weight of, 57^9; as standard of weight (??), 57^9-58^9.

Coincidences of P:, 83^{1-4}; for further—see special heads of.

Columbus, Christopher, predicted discovery of America by, in the "ruled lines" (?), 46^9.

Commission, Fr. Sci., measures of side of base of P: by, 18^8-19^4; report of Imperial, on M. S. in W. and Cen. Europe in 1876, 3^8.

Committee on coinage, weights and measures in U. S. recommend use of M. S., 3^8; Joint, of Royal Soc. of London and Fr Acad. of Sci. to determine a basis of system of weights and measures, 2^9.

Connecticut favored M. S. by legislation, 3^9-4^1.

Constantine, date of accession of to power predicted by P: (?), 44^9.

Constantinople, capture of, predicted by "ruled lines" of P: (?), 46^4.

Constituent Assembly, action of, in regard to adoption of a universal system of weights and measures, 2^8.

Cornu, Mr., experiment of, to determine velocity of light, 33^9.

Crusade, date of first, predicted by "ruled lines" (?), 46^4.

Cubit, derivation of, 1^7; dissertation on by Sir I. Newton, 27^{6-9}; double-rule of Karnak, 30^{6-9}; value of Karnak rule in Brit. in., 30^8; identical with P: unit of base measure, 27^3-31^7; investigations of value of, 27^{6-9}; real value of, 30^{1-3}; sacred (??), 28^1, 28^9-29^1; mentioned in Bible, 28^4-30^9.

Custom House in Russia, use of M. S. ordered in, 3^9.

Date, of construction of P:, 14^8-16^6; of Theater, 88^{6-7}; of Adam, 38^1; of deluge, 37^6-38^8; of the exodus, 38^8-39^9; of the dispersion, 38^{1-9}; of the annunciation, 39^9-40^8.

Denon and Jombard, imputation of error to, by Smyth, 84^9.

Density of Earth, methods of finding, 51^{7-9}; results of, 52^{1-4}.

Diagram of P:, 9^{1-9}; to illustrate batter of P:, 79^{6-7}.

Diana, Temple of, 83^9-89^3.

Diet of Worms, prediction of date of, by "ruled lines" (?), 46^4.

Digit, derivation of, 1^7: P:, 50^8.

Doctrine of P: (??), 7^1-17^8; evolution of, of divine inheritance of weights and measures (??), 4^9; orthodox, on height of P: (??), 31^{6-9}.

Dove, Prof., determination of latitude of mean temperature of earth by, 63^4; on mean temperature of earth, 71^9; of Nile Delta, 71^9.

Draconis, Alpha, pole-star of P., 14^4-16^6; position of 4,000 years ago, 15^6.

Earth, circumference of, determined by Eratosthenes, 23^7-24^5; daily motion of, expressed in P: in (??), 8^1; math. relations bet. daily motion of and P: units (??), 35^3-36^9; density of, 51^7-52^4; distance of from sun a multiple of P: height (??), 31^3-32^3; figure of, 24^4-25^1; globular figure of, not known to Egyptians, 62^{6-7}; specific gravity of, implicitly determined by P: coffer (??), 14^{1-9}, 57^9-58^5; polar axis of, 24^8-27^9.

Eastern Empire, prediction by "ruled lines" of downfall of (?), 46^4.

Egypt, Lower, center of habitable land (??), 13^9; ignorance of geography outside of, on part of ancient Egyptians, 63^9.

Ell, derivation, 1^7; value of lunar, 85^9; division of (?), 87^{1-3}; a function of linear measures; of P: (?), 89⁴–91³; of Odeon (?), 87⁷–88¹; of Temple (?), 87⁸; of Theater (?), 87⁷.

Encke, computation of solar distance by, 32⁷.

England, failure to adopt M. S. in, 3³.

Ephesus, 83⁶–89⁸; explorations in, by Mr. J. T. Wood, 84¹⁻⁵.

Eta Tauri, astronomical relations of, to P:, 15⁷.

Eratosthenes, determination of earth's circumference by, 23⁸–24⁸.

Everest, Col., Director of Indian Meridian Survey, 25⁶⁻⁹.

Exodus of Israelites, date of, predicted by "ruled lines" (??), 46⁹.

Fiveness, principle of (??), 58³; of P: proportions (??), 16⁶; of P: thermometric scale (??), 71⁴; sacred to Ephesians (?), 87⁸.

Fizeau and *Foucault*, experimental determination of velocity of light by, 33⁴.

Foot measures, derivation, 2⁸; number of different, 2⁶.

Foucault and *Fizeau*, experimental determination of velocity of light by, 33⁴.

Geographical position of P:, 12⁸, 64¹⁻³, 69⁴.

George IV., bushel and quarter under, 54⁹–55³.

Gizeh hill, latitude of, 64¹⁻³; most land under meridian of (??), 69⁸.

Gliddon, Geo. R., reference to "Types of Mankind" by, on date of the annunciation, 40⁶.

Gravity, Specific, of earth an implicit function of the capacity of the coffer of P: (??), 14¹⁻³, 57⁸–58⁵.

Great Pyramid, the. See Pyramid.

Greaves, Prof. John, a translation by, on cubits, 27⁶.

Greswell, date of the annunciation by, 40⁸.

Guyot's Meteorological maps, isotherm of Egypt in, 63⁸.

Hales, tables of dates of the annunciation by, 40⁸; date of deluge by, 37⁹; of the exodus, 39⁷; of birth of Solomon by, 45⁹.

Height of P: (??), 31⁸–32⁸; a function of solar distance (??), 8¹⁻⁹. See P.

Henry I., determination of yard length from arm of, 53⁸.

Henry III., primitive history of weights and measures in reign of, 53⁷.

Henry VI., Winchester bushel in reign of, 54⁸.

Henry VII., value of bushel in reign of, 54³; change of value of bushel under, 54⁴.

Henry VIII., value of bushel in reign of, 54⁵.

Herodotus, quoted; on acts of Shepherd Kings, 64⁸; on time and work of building P:, 6³; on inscription upon exterior of P:, 41⁷; by Smyth, 67¹⁻⁸.

Herostratus, destruction of Temple of Diana by, 83⁴.

Herschel, Sir J., results of meridian arc measurements by, 26⁸; method of in determining the pole-star at foundation of P:, 75⁴⁻⁵.

HISTORIQUES, *L'Art de verifier les Dates des Faits*, date of the annunciation given in, 39⁹–40¹; of the deluge, 37⁹; of the dispersion, 38⁹; of the exodus, 38⁹.

Hug and *Pearson*, date of the annunciation by, 40⁹.

Hyksos Rule in Lower Egypt, 67²; of middle dynasties, 67⁶.

Hyperbolic system of logarithms, theory of, as a condition for determining *a priori* the P: base (?), 94¹–95³.

Inches, British, relation of to P: unit of external measures (??), 24⁸–27²; P:, assumed value of (??), 7⁷.

Inclination of P: significance of, (??) 11¹⁻⁴; of different passages in P. (??), 76³⁻⁴. See P.!

Ideler, date of the annunciation by, 40⁸.

Inglis, observations on corner sockets by, 76⁶⁻⁷; *and Aiton*, object of, in visiting Gizeh, 20⁶.

Inheritance, divine, doctrine of, of weights and measures (? ?), 4⁶⁻⁹; "Our — in the P:" quoted, 11³, 12⁸–13³, 18⁴⁻⁵, 32²⁻³, 39¹, 49⁴⁻⁵, 49³–50³, 67³–68³, 90¹⁻⁴.

Institute, International, for preserving and perfecting weights and measures, 4³, 6⁶.

Intellectual Man, antiquity of, quoted, 34⁸–35¹, 35³⁻⁵.

Interchange of articles of personal property, 1.

Introduction of M. S. in Eng., 3⁶.

Isis, worship of, influence upon builders of the Temple (?), 85⁴⁻⁸, 86⁸; upon builders of P:, 90⁸, 91³.

Isotherm of 30° lat. not that of earth, 63⁸⁻⁹.

Israelites, exodus of, from Egypt predicted by the "ruled lines" (??), 37³, 38⁸–39⁶.

Jackson, date of deluge by, 37⁹; of exodus, 39¹.

James', *Col. Sir Henry*, method of finding earth's density, 51⁶; results, 52¹; building process of P: suggested by, 81¹⁻⁴.

Jeeueh, *P.*, date of erection, 67¹.

Jerusalem, predicted capture of, by "ruled lines" (?), 46⁸; built by Philitis, 67⁴.

Joktan and brothers, builders of P: (??), 6³.

Jomard and *Denon*, imputation of error to, by Smyth, 84.⁸

Karnak, double-cubit rule of, 30⁴⁻⁵; a measure of capacity of coffer of P:, 51¹; value in Brit. in., 30⁸, an exact measure of sides and passages of P:, 30⁸–31³; variation of royal cubit from, 61⁴⁻⁷.

Khufu, King (*Suphis. Cheops*), erector of P: according to Vyse, 6¹.

Lamy, date of the annunciation by, 40⁸.

Latitude of P: (? ?), 62³–64⁸; not 30°, 63⁴–64⁴; object in choice of, 12⁶.

Legation, "Theory of the Divine, of P:," 7³.

Legislation on Brit. weights and measures, 53¹–55⁶.

Length, coffer a standard of (??), 58⁸–59³; questions of, 1¹⁻⁵. See P:.

Lepsius, date of exodus by, 38³–39¹.

Leverrier, parallax assumed by, 33¹

Light, solar distance determined by velocity of, 33⁴⁻⁷; velocity of determined, 33⁴⁻⁷.

Linear Measure, unit of (? ?), 17⁸–20³.

Lines, Ruled, theory of (? ?), 44⁸; author's theory of (?), 45¹⁻⁶.

Lippeman, date of the annunciation by, 40⁷.

Location of P:, special Providence in (? ?), 13⁴.

Logarithms, common system of, function of coffer (?), 59⁷–61⁸; Petrie's measurements preclude the theory of, 94¹–95¹; Napierian, 59³–61⁸; Hyperbolic system of, theory of as an *a priori* condition for determining the P: base (?), 94¹–95¹.

Longitude of P:, importance of (? ?), 68³–69³; object of (??), 12⁵; metrological (? ?), 64⁸; reasons for choice of (? ?), 64⁴–69⁸; a standard meridian (??), 13⁴.

Longitudinal dimensions of passages of P:, meaning of (? ?), 36⁸–46⁸.

Louis XVI., connection of, with metrological movement, 2⁸.

Lunar Ell, 85⁸; division of (?), 87¹⁻³; function of breadth of Temple (?), 87⁸; of length of Temple (?), 86⁴⁻⁷; of linear measures of P: (?), 89⁴–91⁸.

Lunar Metron, 89⁴; function of breadth of K. C. (?), 89⁸.

Lunar Theory of P: (?), 83³–91⁸; urged acceptance of (?), 91⁴⁻⁵.

Lunation, connection of with linear measures of the Temple (?), 85$^{2-4}$; connection of mean, with diameter of Theater (?), 88$^{2-3}$.
Luther, Reformation of, predicted in P: (?), 43^5.
Lyræ, Alpha, 15^3.
Lysimachus, reconstruction of Temple by, 83$^{7-9}$.

Magnan, Father, date of the annunciation by, 40^4.
Mahomet II., capture of Constantinople by, predicted in "ruled lines" (?), 46^4.
Mamoun, Al, connection of, with P: and coffer, 47^9–49^3.
Manasseh, date of liberation of, 46^1.
Manetho, fragments of, 64^7.
"*Mankind, Types of*," reference to, on date of the annunciation, 40^6.
Maskelyne's method of finding earth's density, 51^9; results, 52^1.
Masonry Core of P:, 78^7.
Massachusetts, M. S. favored by legislation of, 3^9–4^1.
Mass, ratio of total of P: to total of earth (? ?), 14$^{2-3}$.
Measurements of side of base of P:, 19^4; methods for making, 21^9–22^9; why not made? 20^4–23^1; of P:, 20$^{4-8}$; by Vyse, 45$^{2-4}$.
Measures, of P:, 40^9–42^4; of coffer, of capacity of, 60^4; by Smyth, 57$^{1-3}$; number of different foot, 2^8; of inclinations of nine entrance passages of P. by Vyse, 77$^{2-5}$; of length, 1^9; linear, and dates, coincidences of (?), 42^8–45^1; by Petrie, 92^9–94^4; by Taylor's method (? ?), 23^3–24^3; of Temple (?), 84^9–85^1; unit of extreme of P: in connection with Brit. in. (? ?), 24^4–27^3; by Wood, 84$^{2-3}$; measure, P: unit of, identical with cubit (? ?), 27^4–31^9; P: unit of, a function of earth's daily motion (? ?), 34^9–36^6; history of systems of weights and, 53^7–55^9; sides and passages of P: exactly measured by Karnak Rule, 30^9–31^3.
Measuring Rule, discovery and description of (?), 85^9–86^9; sacred (?), 86$^{3-4}$.
Melchizedek, identical with Philitis (? ?), 67^9–68^9; limits of geographical knowledge of, 69^7.
Meridian, measurements of, arcs, 24^9–27^3; determination of axis of earth by Airy from mean of measurements of, 26^7; by Bessel, 26^7; greater Azimuthal error of Uranienborg, than P:, 71^8; of P:, 69^9, 13^1; measurements by Sir J. Herschel, 26^6; different, 69^8–69^9.
Meridian line, simple method for determining, 74$^{2-4}$; of Paris, 3^1; Proctor's method for determination of a (? ?), 73^7–74^1; measures under Gen. de Schubert, 25^9–26^1; limited signification of in P: theory, 69^4; from Syene to Alexandria, 23^9.
Metre, adoption and signification of, 2^8; a basic unit, 3^1.
Metric System, adoption of, 3^3; use of in custom houses ordered in Russia, 3^3; in Conn., Mass., N. J., 3^9–4^1; Barnard's, 2^4; in Eng., 3$^{2-7}$; in U. S., 3^7.
Metrology in G. B., 55$^{2-3}$; how founded, 53^7.
Metrological System, of P: not beneficial, 66$^{7-9}$; of coffer (? ?), 59$^{2-3}$; theory of, of P: (? ?), 6^5.
Metron, lunar, signification of, 89^4; function of breadth of K. C. (?), 89^9; employed in P: (?), 91^9; relation of a quarter of, to P: dimensions, 89^6–90^1, 90^9–91^9.
Michelson, Lieut., determination of velocity of light by, 33$^{6-7}$.
Migration of P: builders (? ?), 67^9.
Mineptah II., Pharaoh of Exodus, 39^7.
Moigno, Abbé, quoted, 90^1–90^6.
Moon, diameter of (?), 85$^{4-7}$; relation to length of Temple (?), 86^9–87^1.
Muller, editor of "Alphonsine Tables," 40^7.

Napier, Baron, discovery of hyperbolic system of logarithms by, 95^1; discovery of antedated by P: builders (?), 61$^{7-8}$.

Newcomb, Prof., on density of earth, 52^2; on solar distance, 34^1.
New Jersey, M. S. favored by legislation of, 3^2-4^1.
Newton, Sir Isaac, dissertation of, on cubits, 27^{6-8}.
Noah, date of birth of, 38^1; originator of P: (? ?), 5^4-6^2.
Number, measure of quantity, 1; numbers of special prominence in P: (? ?), 16^5-17^4; in the Temple (?), 87^{1-4}.

Object of builders of P: (? ?), 59^2-61^2. See P.
Odeon, 84^6; diameter of, determined, 87^7; measure of, by Wood, 84^6; curious relations implied in (?), 87^5-88^2.
Orientation of P:, 14^4, 71^5-72^8; error in, 72^1; relation of inclination of passage to, 72^2-73^8; object in, 72^{3-6}; simple method for, 72^3, 74^{2-4}.

Palm, an Egyptian, 94^{1-2}.
Parallax, determined by Airy, 32^2; assumed by Leverrier, 33^1; solar, recent determinations of, 32^6-33^2; solar distance determined by, 32^6-34^3; from observations, 32^3.
Passage, astronomical significance of ascending — and grand gallery of P: (? ?), 15^5-16^3; lengths determined (? ?), 10^4. See P:.
Paulus, date of the annunciation by, 40^6.
Pearson and *Hug*, date of the annunciation by, 40^2.
Peleg, date of birth of, 38^3.
Perring, measures of side of base of P: by, 19^4.
Petavius, date of annunciation by, 40^5; of deluge, 37^9; of exodus, 39^1.
Petrie, Sir Wm., height of P: by (? ?), 31^5-32^2; referred to, 34^9-35^4; W. M. Flinders—object of in visit to Gizeh, 92^3; P: training of, 92^3; "Researches on P:" quoted, 92^{4-9}; results of investigations of, 92^6; "work on PP. and Temples of Gizeh" overthrows P: religion, 91^5-92^1; work of at P:, 92^5-94^6.
Philiton or Philitis, 67^6, 68^{5-7}.
Pi Pyramid, P: apparently a, 80^4-81^6, 17^{4-6}.
Pleiades, position of, when α Drac. was pole star, 15^6-16^6.
Pliny, dimensions of Temple by, 84^6.
Polar Axis, determinations of, 24^7-27^9.
Pole Star, of P:, α Drac. 14^6-16^6; time of passing axis of passage of P: by, 75^1-76^9; Herschel's method of finding, 75^{1-8}.
Post-offices and Custom-houses, use of M. S. in, 3^1.
Postscript, 91^9-95^9.
Pound Weights, derivation, 2^9; number of different, 2^9.
Precessional Year, marked by P: (?), 15^5-16^3.
Proctor's theory of inclination of P: passages, 74^6-75^2; of determination of meridian, 73^{1-6}; (?), 73^7-74^1; of reason for orientation of P:, 72^6; of doctrine of P: religion, 6^7.
Pyramid: (? ?), 82^9-83^4; advent foreshadowed in (? ?), 43^1; implicit quadrature of circle in floor of (?), 89^9-90^1; archæology of (? ?), 40^9-42^9; astron. advantages of (? ?), 72^9; astron. signification of (? ?), 71^5-78^9; of passages of (? ?), 15^6-16^5; base of connected with hyperbolic system of logarithms (?), 94^{1-2}; base measures of (? ?), 7^9; (? ?), 19^4, 18^9; (? ?), 20^6-23^1; proportions of batter of (?), 79^1-80^9; benefit of (? ?), 66^{3-6}; builders of P:, 5^4-6^9; divine mission of (? ?), $12^{5\,7}$; a migratory tribe, 67^9; consistency of (? ?), 49^6-50^3; object of (? ?), 59^9-61^9; practical rule of (?), 81^{3-6}; climatology (? ?), 13^{6-8}, 62^9-63^9; coffer, see under Coffer; coincidences of (?), 36^5-46^6, 42^6-43^1, 43^2-44^9; (? ?), 81^9-82^6, 83^{2-4}; P: date of (? ?), 14^9-16^6, 75^9-76^2; by Barnard, 75^9; by Herschel, 75^7; date of North

Stone — of Dashour, 77⁸; fourth — 77⁷⁻⁸; dates of (? ?), 37¹⁻²; diagram of, 9¹⁻⁹, 79²⁻⁷; — digits, 50⁸; fiveness of (? ?), 16⁸; "The Great," quoted, 5⁴⁻⁵; by Proctor, quoted, 73¹⁻⁸; geographical position of (? ?), 12⁸; height of (? ?), 8¹⁻⁹; 31⁹⁻32³; astron. signif. of inclinations of passages of (? ?), 76³⁻78⁸; difference in (?), 76⁴⁻⁸; prophecy in (? ?), 11⁶⁻¹; alteration in, 76⁸,⁹; how determined, 78⁶⁻⁷, 75⁸; inclination of entrance passages of, 76⁹, 77⁸, 78²⁻³: Proctor's theory of incl. of, 74⁶⁻⁷; angular slope of side of P :, 80⁸⁻81¹; "Our Inheritance in P:" quoted, 11³, 12⁹⁻13³, 18⁴⁻⁶, 32²⁻³, 39⁴, 49⁴⁻⁶, 49⁹⁻50³, 67³⁻68³, 90¹⁻⁸; latitude of, see Latitude; lengths of (? ?), 10⁴; differences in lengths of (?), 90⁷⁻⁸; "Life and Work of P:" quoted, 11⁴, 20⁸, 45⁶; ruled lines of (?), 45¹⁻46⁵; (? ?), 44⁸⁻44⁹, see Longitude; ratio of mass of, to mass of earth (? ?), 14⁴⁻⁶; math. relations of a π P., 34⁴⁻⁵; see Measure; meridian of, 13¹; connected with lunar metron (?), 89⁴⁻91⁸; — numbers (? ?), 16⁸⁻17¹; observations on floor levels of cor. sockets, 76⁶⁻⁷; orientation of, 71⁸⁻72⁸; (? ?), 14⁶, error in, 72¹; incl. of passages in, 72⁹⁻73⁸; passages of P: as measures of time (? ?), 10⁹⁻11⁴; proportions of entrance passages of first four —, 78⁸⁻79¹; P: a π P, 80⁸⁻81⁸; pole star of P., 14⁴⁻⁹, 75⁸⁻76⁷; — pound (? ?), 58¹⁻⁶; a mark of precessional year (? ?), 15⁹⁻16⁶; object of P: (? ?), 5¹; location (? ?), 12⁴⁻⁸; negative — (?), 42¹; according to Taylor (? ?), 65³⁻66⁹; object in passages of P: not astron. (?), 78¹⁻⁴; of 2d P. (?), 77¹⁻⁵; religion of P:(? ?), 6⁷; (?), 91³, 92¹; "Researches on P:" quoted, 92¹⁻⁵; robbery of for building Cairo, 21⁶; situation of (? ?), 14⁴⁻⁷; (? ?), 62³⁻64⁴; time of building P:, 6¹; time of founding So. stone P. of Dashour, 77⁹⁻78¹; no testimony upon P: bequeathed (?), 42²⁻¹; temperature of (? ?), 63¹⁻², 69⁹⁻71⁸; theory of (? ?), 7¹⁻17⁸; (? ?), 17⁹⁻82⁸; 4⁴⁻5¹, 7⁷, 6⁶⁻7¹; crucial test of, 22⁸⁻23¹; new theory of (?), 83⁸⁻91⁹; unit of, of capacity (? ?), 52⁴; of measure (? ?), 27²⁻31²; (? ?), 18⁶⁻20⁸; aliquot part of earth's daily motion (? ?), 8⁹; of polar axis (? ?), 27¹⁻²; (? ?), 7¹; identical with cubit of exodus (? ?), 7⁴⁻⁶; relation between and Brit. in. (? ?), 24⁶⁻27³; of weight the P. ton (? ?), 57³, 58¹⁻⁶; P. units almost identical with our own units, 6⁸; calculation of vol. and weight of, by Smyth, 5⁸.

Quarter, signification of, 53²⁻⁴; value of in cu. in., 54⁹; variation in values of, 53⁹⁻55⁷.

Regiomontanus, 40⁷.
Reich, method for finding earth's density, 51⁸; results, 52¹.
Religion of P:. See P. (?), 90⁶, 91¹.
Roman Empire, date of rise and fall of predicted in P: (?), 43⁹⁻44⁶.
Rome, capture and burning of, by Brennus predicted by "ruled lines" (?), 46⁸; foundation of (?), 46².
Russia, failure to adopt M. S., 3⁷.

Saladin, Saracen Sultan, predicted capture of Jerusalem by, in "ruled lines" (?), 46⁶.
Sanclemente, date of the annunciation by, 40⁸.
Sarcophagus, the coffer a, 46⁹⁻47⁴.
Scaliger, date of the annunciation by, 40⁹.
Schubert, Gen. de, results of meridian survey under, 25⁹⁻26⁸.
Septuagint, Alexandrian codex of, on date of dispersion, 38⁷; of exodus, 39⁹; Vatican codex of, on date of deluge, 37⁷.
Seven, the number sacred to Ephesians (?), 87⁸.
Shepherd Kings, mentioned, 64⁹; acts of, mentioned in Herodotus, 64⁸; hatred of, 64⁹⁻65¹, 66⁹⁻68³; connection of, with P: (? ?), 67¹⁻³.

INDEX.   105

Shofo, King, under control of Philitis (? ?), 67^7.
Solar distance, 32^7–34^1.
Solomon, date of, 45^9.
Smith, dates of annunciation by, 40^9.
Smyth's Piazzi, corroboration of Vyse's determination of angular slope of P:, 80^9; "Antiquity of Intellectual Man," 34^9–35^1, $35^{4.5}$; archæology (? ?), 40^9–42^4; batter of P:, 79^9; difficulties in measuring base side of P: (? ?), 21^7-^{5}; inconsistency imputed to builders of P:, $49^{4.5}$, $67^{4.5}$; *rationale* of — process in computing unit of capacity (? ?), 52^4–53^1; chronology of P: (? ?), 30^9; (? ?), 38^9; (? ?), 75^9–76^2; quoted on climatology of P: (? ?), $13^{4.8}$; formula for capacity of coffer (? ?), 52^4; measures of coffer (? ?), $57^{1.3}$; (? ?), 50^9–53^1; dates of the (? ?), annunciation, 40^6; deluge, 38^9; dispersion, 38^4; exodus, $39^{4.5}$; theory of "ruled lines" (? ?), $44^{2.3}$; observations of cor. sockets, $76^{4.7}$; peculiar omission (? ?), 20^4–23^1; arguments paraphrased (?), 87^1; theory of *personale* of Philitis (? ?), 67^9–68^3; "Our Inheritance in the Great Pyramid," 11^3, 12^9–13^1, $18^{4.5}$, $32^{1.3}$, 39^4, 49^4–50^3, 67^9–68^3, $90^{1.3}$; Life and Work at the P:," 10^9, 11^4, 45^9; π P. doctrine, $17^{4.8}$; calculations on height of a π P. (? ?), $81^{4.8}$; computation of pole star of P:, $75^{4.5}$; solar distance (? ?), 33^7–34^1; P: thermometric scale (? ?), $71^{4.8}$; *resumé* of — argument about P: unit (? ?), $18^{4.5}$; 17^9–21^9; computations of volume and weight of P:, 5^9.
Standards of capacity, methods of testing, $56^{1.7}$.
Star, α Drac. pole — when P: was built, 14^9–16^8.
Statute, earliest British, upon metrology, 53^9.
Survey, Indian meridian, under Col. Everest, $25^{4.5}$.
Surveyors (ordnance), measurements of side of base of P: by, 19^4.
Suskind, date of the annunciation by, 40^9.
Syene, meridian of, 23^9.

Tale, transfer of articles by, I.
Talmud, no mention of cubit in, 28^9.
Taylor's, John, capacity of coffer, 51^1; theory of metrology of coffer, $53^{3.6}$; dates of deluge, 38^3; dispersion, 38^4; method of connecting P: with earth's dimensions (? ?), 23^3–24^4; admission of hostility of Egyptians to Shepherd Kings, 64^4; imputed inconsistency, $65^{4.8}$; to P: builders, 49^9–50^3: π property of P: $17^{4.8}$; statement, $65^{2.4}$; object of inhabitants of Shinar (? ?), $65^{1.3}$; object of P: (? ?), 65^4–66^3; P: theory, 5^9.
Temperature, conditions of constant, 69^9–70^9; of $30°$ lat. not mean — of earth, $63^{1.3}$; of P: (? ?), $13^{4.8}$; a standard — (? ?), 69^4–71^4.
Temple of Diana, 83^9–89^3; breadth of (?), $87^{1.3}$; date of destruction of, 83^9, 83^9–84^1; dimensions of, by Pliny, 84^1; length of, a function of moon's diameter (?), 86^9–87^1; length of a multiple of lunar ells (?), $86^{4.7}$; measures of (?), 84^9–85^1; discovery of measuring rule in (?), 85^9–86^9; measures of, by Wood, 84^9; *and Odeon*, curious relations of (?), 87^9–88^3; reconstruction of, 83^7; *and Theatre*, coincidences of (?), $89^{1.3}$.
Testament, Old, Masoretic Hebrew text of on date of deluge, 37^4; Samaritan text on deluge, 37^7.
Theatre, diameter of, 87^7 (?), $88^{4.8}$, 88^9–89^1; measures of, by Wood, 84^9.
Thermometry, no knowledge of, by antiquity (?), 70^9–71^9.
Timaos mentioned, 64^7.
Tropical Year connected with P: (? ?), $18^{4.5}$.
Troy, Siege of, date of, predicted in P: (?), $44^{1.3}$.
Two, number, sacred to Ephesians (?), 87^9.

8

Unit, of capacity (?), 52⁴ ; of length (? ?), 35⁹–36⁸ (?), 7⁴⁻⁸ (?), 17⁸–20⁸, 34⁸–36⁸ ; test of K. C., 89⁶–90¹ ; of weight (? ?), 58¹⁻⁸, 57⁷ ; variations of, 2¹⁻³.

Usher's, Archbishop, dates of deluge, 37⁸ ; dispersion, 38⁷ ; exodus, 39¹ ; of the annunciation, 40⁸.

Veii, predicted capture of, in "ruled lines" (?), 46².

Vyse, Col. Howard, construction of P: by King Khufu acc. to, 6²⁻⁸ ; measurements of angular slope of side of P:, 80⁷ ; of side of base (? ?), 18⁸, 19⁴ ; of inclination of entrance passages of nine Pyramids, 77²⁻⁴, 45²⁻⁴ ; work of, on P:, 10⁸.

Weight, ideality of P: as standard of, 58⁶ ; material of unit of (? ?), 58¹⁻⁸ ; history of weights and measures, 53⁷–55⁹, 2¹, 2³, 2⁹ ; P: ton a unit of, 57⁸ ; how determined, 58¹⁻⁸.

Wiesler, date of the annunciation by, 40⁹.

Wilkins on date of the exodus, 39¹.

William III., Winchester bu. re-established and defined under, 54⁷.

Winchester bushel, 54⁸, 54⁷.

Wood, J. T., explorations of, about Ephesus, 84¹⁻⁶.

Worms, Diet of, predicted by "ruled lines" (?), 40⁸.

Yard, derivation, 1⁷ ; determination of, 53⁷.

Year, precessional (? ?), 15⁸ ; sidereal, connected with Temple, Theatre, Odeon at Ephesus (?), 87⁹–89¹ ; tropical, connected with Odeon (?), 88⁸ ; and base of P: (? ?), 18¹⁻².

Young, determination of solar distance by, 34².

Zephathah, predicted battle in Valley of, (?), 46².

Zerah, defeat of by Asa predicted in "ruled lines" (?), 46¹.

ERRATA.

Page 2, line 17 from bottom, *dele* comma after three.
" 6, " 5 " top, for *brothers* read *sons*.
" 7, " 4 " " *dele* the whole line.
" 7, " 3 " bottom, for 366.2596 read 366.2591.
" 8, " 4 " " *dele the*.
" 9, Right hand side, put in I before Coffer.
" 11, line 14 from top, for *of* read *at*.
" 11, " 14, " Life and Work at the Great Pyramid " should be in italics.
Page 12, line 17 from top, for *evidently* read *possibly*.
" 14, " 5 " " for *probably* read *somewhere near*.
" 17, " 8 " " " Antiquity of Intellectual Man " should be in italics.
Page 18, line 18 from top, insert comma after *base-breadth*.
" 18, " 13 " bottom, place " " to include the sentence beginning with *Evidently* and ending with *building*.
Page 21, last line, for *measured* read *measuring*.
" 22, line 19 from top, for *would* read *could*.
" 22, " 20 " " " *could* read *would*.
" 31, " 14 " " " *one one thousand* read *one one-thousand*.
" 33, 1st line, insert *Mr.* before *Leverrier*.
" 35, line 18 from top, for $10^7 +_4$ read 10^{7+4}.
" 42, " 19 " " insert *be* after *may*.
" 56, " 14 " bottom, for *This* read *The*.
" 67, " 23 " top, after *place*, put ".
" 67, " 11 " bottom, *dele the*.
" 68, " 7 " top, for *Messiamic* read *Messianic*.
" 73, " 2 " " after *direction* insert *and*.
" 78, " 19 " " *dele for* after *been*.
" 80, " 2 " " for 26° 17' read 26° 27'.
" 82, " 15 " " bottom, for *stone like* read *stone of like material with*.
Page 85, line 12 from top, for 14. read 14 *multiplied by ten*.
" 90, " 11 " bottom, for *supposed* read *disposed*.
" 91, " 19 " top, for *a* read *the*.
" 92, " 12 " bottom, after *of* insert *the preface to*.
" 92, " 5 " " after *funeral* insert ".
" 92, " 3 " " for *alive* ' " read *alive*."
" 93, " 1, for *in* read *to*.

www.ingramcontent.com/pod-product-compliance
Lightning Source LLC
Chambersburg PA
CBHW031406160426
43196CB00007B/924